Cambridge Elements ≡

Elements in Ancient Egypt in Context
edited by
Gianluca Miniaci
University of Pisa
Juan Carlos Moreno García
CNRS, Paris
Anna Stevens
University of Cambridge and Monash University

COFFIN COMMERCE

How a Funerary Materiality Formed Ancient Egypt

Kathlyn M. Cooney
University of California Los Angeles

CAMBRIDGE
UNIVERSITY PRESS

CAMBRIDGE
UNIVERSITY PRESS

University Printing House, Cambridge CB2 8BS, United Kingdom

One Liberty Plaza, 20th Floor, New York, NY 10006, USA

477 Williamstown Road, Port Melbourne, VIC 3207, Australia

314–321, 3rd Floor, Plot 3, Splendor Forum, Jasola District Centre,
New Delhi – 110025, India

79 Anson Road, #06–04/06, Singapore 079906

Cambridge University Press is part of the University of Cambridge.

It furthers the University's mission by disseminating knowledge in the pursuit of
education, learning, and research at the highest international levels of excellence.

www.cambridge.org
Information on this title: www.cambridge.org/9781108823333
DOI: 10.1017/9781108913881

First published 2021

A catalogue record for this publication is available from the British Library.

ISBN 978-1-108-82333-3 Paperback
ISSN 2516-4813 (online)
ISSN 2516-4805 (print)

Coffin Commerce

How a Funerary Materiality Formed Ancient Egypt

Elements in Ancient Egypt in Context

DOI: 10.1017/9781108913881
First published online: May 2021

Kathlyn M. Cooney
University of California Los Angeles

Author for correspondence: Kathlyn M. Cooney, cooney@g.ucla.edu

Abstract: This discussion will be centered on one ubiquitous and rather simple Egyptian object type – the wooden container for the human corpse. We will focus on the entire "lifespan" of the coffin – how they were created, who bought them, how they were used in funerary rituals, where they were placed in a given tomb, and how they might have been used again for another dead person. Using evidence from Deir el Medina, we will move through time from the initial agreement between the craftsman and the seller, to the construction of the object by a carpenter, to the plastering and painting of the coffin by a draftsman, to the sale of the object, to its ritual use in funerary activities, to its deposit in a burial chamber, and, briefly, to its possible reuse.

Keywords: Egypt, funerary culture, materiality, coffins, economy

ISBNs: 9781108823333 (PB), 9781108913881 (OC)
ISSNs: 2516-4813 (online), 2516-4805 (print)

Contents

1 Introduction

Egypt is best known – today and in antiquity – for its obsession with things. But not just any things; in our eyes, the Egyptians were obsessed most with those things associated with death. And thus we are to understand that, for the Egyptians, death itself was something to be physically overcome by massive quantities of gold and precious gems, hard stones to make massive sarcophagi, columned tombs hewn from living rock or built out of masonry blocks, fine-grained wood to build body containers, not to mention all of the collected quotidian objects to feed and clothe the deceased in the afterlife, stuffed into the burial chamber with the corpses of the dead. Indeed, our modern world celebrates and visually consumes all of this materiality of Egyptian death within museum spaces, thus constructing an ancient Egypt that was the most material-istic of cultures, and impractical and superstitious to boot.

But what was the reason for all of this death-related materiality? And was Egypt really as death-obsessed as we think? It was Gene Wilder playing Dr. Frankenstein who yelled in the 1974 film *Young Frankenstein*, "I am not interested in death; I am interested in the preservation of life!" At which point he pounds a scalpel into his leg to accentuate his point. Egyptology too is prepared for the logic flip from death to life. Indeed, researchers enable it, denying an Egyptian obsession with mortality, arguing instead that the ancient Egyptians were focused on continuing life (Assmann 2005: 1; Parkinson 2010), thus enabling the scholarly transformation of all those crafted and collected funerary things into "embodiments," that is, symbols of what people would have wanted if they were to live forever, not a literal expectation of physicality in the afterlife. This intellectual turn from "death" to "life" has enabled Egyptology to see every coffin or tomb as a remnant of a social life once lived, as a human reality in which the dead did not bury themselves and in which death objects were representative of human wishes and social status. The living created these objects to manifest particular social powers. And it is the actions and social manifestations of those living at the moment the funerary goods were made, sold, displayed and deposited that were being played out. Summarily stated, funerary actions are, at least in part, documents of social power by living people.

Egypt is known for its obsession with death-related stuff – all of those daily-life objects crammed into tombs, the furniture, wigs, food, dishes, jars, cosmet-ics, sandals, and clothing, not to mention the coffins. It is also true that these things were made to draw our attention, as they were fashioned with shiny metals, bright paints, glossy resins, and eye-catching iconography. These funer-ary objects were created to manufacture social power. We still cannot look away from them, it seems, and Egyptian-based exhibitions regularly cycle in and out of museum spaces to enormous crowds (usually quietly derided by other curatorial staff as yet another Egypt death show that should be abhorred as naive, fetishized, materialistic, etc.).

It seems that the obsession with death, on the one hand, and the obsession with things, on the other, have been conflated to create some negative stereotypes. At the same time that Egyptology examines all things funerary, postprocessual archaeology often treats "things," in and of themselves, as base and primitive, hardly touching those supposedly superior cognitive realms of humanity. And so, we are embarrassed to be seen counting and analyzing these ancient things – even though we are not the ones who deposited them in the first place. The ancient materiality continues to have so much social power that it confounds the research. Funerary materiality was and is such a powerful method of manufacturing social power that it still creates shock and awe within the modern human mind, millennia after it was deposited in a burial.

Many humanistic scholars have been trained that they should be involved only with the mind, the abstract, the intellectual, or, if we must examine the baser materialistic side of humanity, then we should focus on history, social change, dynasties, and power (LeCain 2017). Thus, we are taught that *things*, however we define them, are not something to which we should be giving our precious attention, and, if we do, then we should direct our cerebral focus to the human input those things embody. We prefer to examine things as human manipulations because "[s]ince humans have been in existence we have affected the world on a large scale so all things are to some degree human made artifacts" (Hodder 2012: 4). Such problematic anthropocentrism fits well with the Egyptological mindset because we continue to catalog our excavated objects while prioritizing the thought encoded upon them or embodied within them, seeing funerary things like coffins and tombs only as vehicles for the cognitive information they contain, giving prominence to religion over the material conveyance, to decode the thought patterns of the ancient Egyptians, even though the immaterial could not exist without the material.

We do not want to admit how the material – the stone, wood, plaster, varnish, and pigment – could in fact have agency of its own that can be wielded over the human. Indeed, as I will argue in this Element, these funerary things so cleverly created by the ancient Egyptians ended up creating a genie that they could not put back into the bottle and under whose influence they themselves were quite helpless, unable to abandon the social powers of the material, prone to the power of the funerary things they had "brought to life." Indeed, these funerary objects wielded so much energy over the Egyptian mind that when scarcity set in, people made all kinds of adaptations so that they could continue to acquire them, engaging in recommodification and reuse of already existing funerary things, performing what would previously have been seen as immoral actions, all so that they, too, could benefit from their extraordinary power. Ancient Egyptians never abandoned their death materiality.

Many who study ancient Egypt are drawn to the things not preserved elsewhere – painted and plastered wooden objects, dried fruit, loaves of bread, linen garments, leather sandals, chariots. Egyptologists who surround themselves with materiality in their work often feel the need to cover a perceived materialistic obsession by adding a cognitive veneer – determining what symbols the things represented to the ancient Egyptians, abstract cognition, religious ideas, social realities, human details about identity, and so on. As Olsen observes "No wonder then that the material qualities of things have increasingly been covered up by the piles of epistemologies invented to make them as transparent and compliant as possible, in which their role is never to be themselves" (Olsen 2010: 26).

In some ways, the field of Egyptology has an identity problem. We are like the baseball card collectors of antiquity studies, stereotyped in other fields as antiquarians and connoisseurs, not interested in elucidating the great human condition, but only in collecting more stuff. While the cataloging and typologizing of all that preserved material have encouraged many of us to eschew theoretical archaeology, it is becoming clear that ancient Egyptian datasets create the ideal circumstances to study materialism itself and how it has shaped and continues to shape a human society obsessed with stuff – from ancient coffins and tombs to plastic water bottles, fast fashion, and Amazon Prime.

Egyptology is usually materially grounded in its inquiries, even among the philological side of the field. Egyptology has certainly never been "under-materialized" (Olsen 2010: 26), a fact that could be discomfiting to the researchers themselves, as it unfairly implies that many were drawn to this world of pharaohs and pyramids precisely because of its beautiful objects and the (unspoken) connoisseurship thereof.

But the materiality of Egyptology is its strength. We Egyptologists know tens of thousands of objects in our mind's eye. We know which statues are owned by which museum collections or which were found at which archaeological sites. We look for comparanda constantly. And we categorize. We date. We typologize. We create value judgments, whether we admit it or not, choosing to highlight a few such objects in a given category as masterpieces to be pored over in art history survey volumes, not discarding the vast wealth of ancient materiality considered mediocre or same-y. We separate objects into fine art (such as statues and tomb reliefs) and minor arts (like cosmetic jars and scarabs). We discuss craft specialization – how the objects were commissioned, in what workshops they were made, how they were exchanged, displayed, and interred (Amenta & Guichard 2017; Broekman et al. 2018; Clark 1990; Costin 1991, Costin & Wright 1998; Miniaci et al. 2018). We identify craftsmen's hands, saying who made what (Amenta & Guichard 2017; Cavilier 2017; Keller 1984, 1991, 2001, 2003; Rigault & Thomas 2018). We put these objects into functional types: royal stone statuary, temple reliefs, obelisks, funerary stelae, private statuary, coffins, wooden furniture, jewelry, and so on. We pay extra attention to the materials used to make these objects (sandstone, varnish, red granite, pigment, acacia wood, gypsum plaster, etc.), evaluating each ingredient all the while: was it imported or native; man-made or naturally occurring; costly or cheap?

That materiality wields power over the researcher. Egyptology deals with so much stuff that the field drowns in it. We talk of religious functionality and how it was available to anyone who could emulate the objects of their richer cousins, like an offering bearer that does not come close aesthetically and materially to the brilliantly executed example found in Meketre's tomb (Figure 1 and Figure 2). We might assume that the lesser object performed the same magical functions as the one of greater aesthetic value, but in our synthetic analyses we largely ignore

Figure 1 Offering bearer, Tomb of Meketre, 12th Dynasty. Metropolitan Museum of Art, 20.3.7.

Figure 2 Offering bearer, 12th–13th Dynasty.Metropolitan
Museum of Art, 24.1.1.

those objects without symmetry, balance, or quality of applied line, in favor of the
better made thing. We copy and translate the religious inscriptions from the
objects' surfaces, creating source patternbooks, reveling in our ability to reach
the cognition of people buried thousands of years ago. We discuss iconographic
and semiotic meaning, seeing mastery of order over chaos in a tomb painting in
which the deceased man spears fish in a marshland accompanied by his wife and
children in fancy dress (Figure 3), or understanding multiple divine manifestations of a king shown, somehow, worshipping himself on a temple wall (Figure
4). To do all of this material analysis, we demand better photos, databases,
information about materials used. We Egyptologists are so cognizant of how
much cataloging still needs to be done that only recently have we had the luxury
to come up for air and ask what it all means (Olsen 2010: 11, 23, 98).

Object studies allow us to examine how materiality forms a society – whether
that society consists of a bunch of Egyptologists or a (larger) bunch of ancient
Egyptians, because these thousands upon thousands of well-preserved things
are formative in their own rights. How were the ancient Egyptians themselves
affected by their own preservative climate and its resulting overwhelming

Figure 3 Ramses II worshipping himself in a relief at his temple at Abu Simbel, Egypt. Sunken Relief, Lateral Chamber, Ramses II Temple, 19th Dynasty, UNESCO World Heritage Site, Abu Simbel, Egypt. Photo credit: Richard Maschmeyer/Alamy Stock Photo.

materialism? How did desert aridity, which could preserve a human body intact with flesh, nails, and hair, work upon the ancient Egyptian mind? How did abundant farming and easy access to extraordinary mineral resources and draft labor change the Egyptian intellect and culture? How did objects crafted for the dead make social claims on the living? Wengrow argues that such high cost materiality "gave tangible expression to the person's mobility within, and command over, social space via the material landscapes it encompassed" (Wengrow 2006: 122).

Many of us know in our bones that the ancient Egyptians were also a people of stuff. They were materialistic too. Compared with some of their ancient peers they were even hoarders. We can innately understand them to be such, coming from our own overabundant world of computer-guided factory production in which everything sparks joy and so much stuff is maintained that the United States has almost as many storage units as people (Arnold & Lang 2007; Smith 2019; Strutner 2015).

Scholars of New Materialism, like Tim LeCain, Bjønar Olsen, Nicole Boivin, and to some extent even Ian Hodder, have moved away from the postmodern turn of anthropocentrist views of the world in which human agency is the prime mover of culture and history, in which evolutionary biology – nurture, if you

Figure 4 Nebamun hunting in the marshes with his family. Tomb of
Nebamun, 18th Dynasty, Thebes, Egypt. © Trustees of the British Museum.

will – could never trump culture. Neomaterialist thinking is exactly what can
help us understand the agency of things on the ancient Egyptian mind
(DeMarrais, Gosden & Renfrew 2004; Malafouris 2013). As Tim LeCain states,
"The result will be a new type of history and humanism, one in which we
recognize that history, culture, and creativity arise from the things around us"
and that "humans are not an exception to the material world so much as an
expression of it" (LeCain 2017: 15).

And this is where one ubiquitous Egyptian object type comes into our
discussion – the wooden container for the human corpse. It is the object that
mediates transitions, "transforming the body into an image," which, as David
Wengrow argues for mummification, was a means of "extending the period
between death and burial, and treating the body as image and sign" (Wengrow
2006: 123). A close examination of the Egyptian coffin from creation, sale,
religious transformation, deposition, theft, and reuse (Cooney Forthcoming-b)
can help us to understand how we humans are animals shaped by the material
world around us (LeCain 2017: 38). In this Element, I will argue that materials
and materiality worked on the Egyptian mind as much as the Egyptian mind

worked upon them. The Egyptians were a unique product of all of their stuff, of both natural things like wood and gold and manufactured things like coffins and tombs.

2 The Power of the Thing

Egypt presents us with an extraordinary case study of objectified power. The Egyptian desert environment naturally allowed the preservation of a whole lot of stuff that would easily rot and break down elsewhere, especially organic materials. Egyptian geography created a stark dichotomy between preservative places – deserts and caves – and rotting places – the marshes and Nile Valley. Egypt was the land of the mummy for a reason; aridity allowed natural preservation that must have seemed an *active* agency to the ancient mind, as if the land itself could maintain a forever physical presence of objects within it that did not decay.

This notion of preserving the dead human body did not spring unaided into one particular Egyptian human's mind, to be forever after embraced and replicated by others who witnessed this first miracle of preservation. Mummification was, instead, only possible as an extension of Egypt's environment, particularly its deserts where extraordinary preservation occurs naturally with no human intervention whatsoever. It was this environment that created a cascade of notions connected to eternal corporeality. In other parts of the world where rain falls, mummification could not become culturally present; in such places we might see people choose to bury their dead in the wet ground with the intention of allowing bodily decay, or they might choose cremation of the corpse with its quick and visible bodily breakdown into ash. Environment plays an active part in cultural development of mortuary belief and ritual. By extension, the objects made within that environment have real power over human culture.

Bruno Latour states, "Consider things, and you will have humans. Consider humans, and you are by that fact interested in things" (Boivin 2008: 177–8; Latour & Porter 1993). Or we can look to Michel Serres who sees objects and the use of them as the main difference between human society and animal society (Serres 1995: 87). The object negotiates our social bonds. And it is essential to see the Egyptian coffin in this way, as an object that has changed the human approach to certain problems, like death, decay, and loss. Or, if we take into account objects we have around us today, like washing machines, we see that such inventions allow us to forego squatting by a river beating our garments upon rocks. In the same way, the coffin allowed the ancient Egyptians to delegate certain tasks, like transformation of the dead into a divinized and communicable form. And so, like the washing machine that makes our clothes clean, the coffin economizes the time and activity needed to continuously awaken, transform, and connect to the dead. The coffin was a stand-in for a series of time-consuming human rituals, its decorations and inscriptions representing a cognitively collected object power. Because the stakes of the actions provided by a coffin were so high (clothes can be cleaned again, but transformation of the dead can ostensibly only be done once and within a limited amount of time before decay set in), the coffin is entangled, fetishized, powerful, personalized, "sticky" in its meanings and associations, so sticky that the Egyptian coffin has power seemingly coming from its own side with, once crafted, unintended consequences of its own (Boivin 2008: 174–5; Cowan 1983).

2.1 Coffins as Social Objects

On the surface, a coffin seems an uncomplicated object that all humanity could share – because all humans die and all humans want to separate the dead from the spaces of the living. But the Egyptian coffin marked a particularly special human corpse that was treated so as not to decay. The decorated coffin broadcast which humans benefited from non-decay of the corpse. Not all Egyptians had access to the disposable income needed to craft a coffin, let alone to mummify a body. To have a coffin was to enter a "restricted sumptuary world" (Wengrow 2006: 144). The coffin in and of itself was a social separator. Some had them; most did not. The coffin was also a social indicator. Some deserved them; some did not.

The Egyptian coffin was used by society to divide those who lived forever in splendor within a divine communicable state and those who did not, separating those who became Osiris and those who became something else. The Egyptian coffin was the ultimate denial that human beings are organic animals, matter meant to return to the earth. The coffin advertised which bodies would not rot when they joined again with sand or mud. The coffin became a container for massive amounts of imported resin, elite conspicuous consumption displayed in rituals when priests liberally poured jar after jar of the precious stuff onto the mummy. Certain woods and resins have inherent anti-fungal and anti-bacterial properties, which were prized by those who could access them. Thus sycamore fig, acacia, and, of course, imported cedars and firs, were treasured for coffin production; ubiquitous palm wood was not. Natron salts are inherently desiccative and industries in support of their exploitation grew in Egypt's western deserts. All of these activities were part of the coffin's function to turn an otherwise soft and decaying body into a divine effigy of forever presence.

The crafting of mummies, coffins, and tombs formed Egyptian society's view of the dead, and, by extension, of the divine. Coffins created controllable and rewardable ancestors for the few. Initially such ancestors were only strongmen – male leaders and close family. Ultimately, social access broadened as the balance of kingship and elite worked itself out. But the ability of a mere few to acquire scarce resources for the afterlife while others could not was essential to the formation of Egyptian economy, religion, and ideology, driving the construction of pyramids, sprawling necropolises, manufacturing public and visible rituals for special ancestors, and shaping understandings of what those ancestors could do for the living.

The coffin was a product of the "extended mind" of an intellectual elite, in which external aids were used to project one human's ritual ability onto countless others, working over time and space, collecting and adding know-ledge over generations (Clark & Chalmers 1998: 7–19; LeCain 2017: 112). In the Egyptian funerary world, the extended human mind created the Pyramid Texts from oral rituals, which stretched into the Coffin Texts, and then the Book of the Dead, and then the Underworld Books, and so on. The extended mind created the various iterations and styles of Egyptian coffins through time, adding and removing elements with a seeming teleological intent.

Some ancient Egyptians belonged to the society of the materialized extended mind; most were excluded to watch from the sidelines, participating only in what could be orally safeguarded, emulated, and copied. In the same way that some academics today cannot do proper research because they lack access to wealthy libraries – digital or physical – elite Egyptians cornered the market on literary education, funerary knowledge, ritual, religious thought, and temple spaces. And they monopolized the materials to make funerary things – the wood, minerals, resins. This extended mind worked with things, engaging with those functional and scarce commodities to reify social power. The coffin was one product of elite extended mind reified in physicality. As such, the coffin is indeed a remnant of living society, not a dead one. It was used to mark social place and enact human competition with one another. The coffin, and by extension the dead themselves, were manipulated by living people to manifest social value.

The Egyptian coffin was marked and individualized with names and images in paint. The complex decoration of Egyptian coffins changed through time, sometimes becoming more complicated, sometimes less, and Egyptologists have provided dense seriation typologies of coffins for the 3000 years in which they were made (Aston 2009; Barwik 1999; Ciampini 2017; Cooney 2014a; Elias & Lupton 2019; Grajetzki 2007; Kanawanti 2005; Myśliwiec 2014; Niwiński 1988; Peterková Hlouchová 2017; Taylor 1989; Willems

1988). Some contemporary coffins were fancier than others, but each was created as a physical construct of social place. The coffin had a material origin in scarce resources, all of which were evocative of the human power to exploit non-human things to create something that – materially or socially or religiously – enhanced the human. Some coffins were more beautiful to look upon, crafted by artisans with more skill and support; some were made with more expensive materials, brought into Egypt over long distances or produced in factories with secret recipes. Coffins are manifestations of human power. We can accept that fact easily; what we do not easily acknowledge is that this materiality shaped the Egyptians in turn. Coffins were a social trap.

I am not trying to take a hard Marxist tack here, blaming objects like coffins for social woes and inequalities (though one certainly could). As Olsen remarks, "Things were increasingly seen as a threat against authentic human and social values, as tellingly manifested in the Marxist (and social-theorist) vocabulary of 'objectification,' 'reification,' and 'instrumental reason'" (Olsen 2010: 12). Coffins were indeed visual markers of social separation, but the coffins themselves were not the underlying reason for that social inequality within ancient Egypt.

2.2 Coffins and Material Consumption

The coffin created unintended consequences for ancient Egyptian society that, once created, manifested a domino effect. Elite Egyptians had to get resources to build the coffin, to decorate it, to display it, to benefit from the object's social power. The mass of Egyptian society who could afford nothing beyond subsistence made do with palm rib matting to contain, embody, and transform their dead. Materiality of containment and nesting was, it seems, essential for all levels of society, but the poor were barred from the scarce resources, forcing them to turn instead to the easily available. The rich found themselves in a bind. They had to access wood, which was scarce in Egypt, maybe from the Delta, if that is where acacia and sycomore fig stands were cultivated, maybe from the Lebanon, vis-à-vis a royal monopoly on fir and cedar. If no such wood was available, the Egyptians created other technologies for body containers, including cartonnage, a papier mâché of linen and plaster, or kiln-baked pottery coffins that demanded charcoal to bake the terracotta. And if scarcity set in, because none of these materials were available, the Egyptian elite turned to theft and reuse to get at the social power that only a coffin could provide.

Material crisis created a situation in which old and interred coffins became valuable commodities that one could refashion, turning the ancestral graveyards into places of coffin harvest, making them insecure and unsafe for new

depositions of the dead and causing people to turn away from old burial grounds
in search of more protected places for their family members, like walled temples
or secret and unmarked caches that they hoped would stay undisturbed. In time
periods of scarcity, the race for materials meant that people could not visit their
loved ones in the necropolis on important calendar dates, like the Theban
Beautiful Feast of the Valley, or whatever ritual of ancestral connection existed
in one's local Egyptian town. Such scarcity would thus change the very nature
of the Egyptian temple, turning many of them into communal places for the
living to congregate and connect with their dead. In other words, the value of
coffin materiality for social standing was so powerful that it created a cascading
causal sequence that reconfigured Egyptian ideas about morality, ancestral
connection, the proper use of burial grounds, and even altered the *raison
d'être* and accessibility of the Egyptian temple itself (Cooney 2011).

Appadurai's studies of human consumption examine how goods are actively
used in social and individual self-creation and in which "things have no
meanings apart from those that human transactions, attributions, and motiv-
ations endow them with" (Appadurai 1986: 5; see also Douglass & Isherwood
1979). But coffins are not valuable just because of their exchange or sign value.
Olsen succinctly puts it thus, "[o]bjects are turned into signs and consumed as
signs; their importance is their sign-value" (Olsen 2010: 32). I am not saying
that Egyptians did not use coffins as attributes, but they also connected with the
coffin's materiality, in and of itself, and were controlled by it in turn.
Anthropologist Alfred Gell is more useful here. He focuses not on the dichotomy between the person and thing, but on the blurred connection between the
two, on the "doing" that connects humans and things, allowing things to thus
have agency over humans, to affect and change people (Gell 1998; Olsen 2010:
135–6). Gell uses the analogy of the soldier being an extension of all his
weaponry and collected emotions that come from his actions with that weaponry (Gell 1998: 21–2). The coffin could become an extension of the person
buried within it, as well as of the people who purchased it, of the religious belief
of the time, the enacted ritual, the priest who performed it, or of the craftsman
who made the coffin in the first place. According to Gell, a coffin could
represent a kind of "distributed personhood" – an extended identity of all
potential actors on the thing. In this way, the Egyptian coffin can be seen as
crafted and controlled by humans for certain social actions, but once the object
was crafted, once those rituals were underway, people were then controlled and
acted upon by the existence of the coffin itself.

Latour's Actor Network Theory is also useful in this regard (Hawary 2018;
Latour & Woolgar 1986). There is a power to coffins. This object combines
wood wealth, mineral wealth, resins and varnishes, containment and nesting,

knowledge of iconography and religious texts, all things that are scarce and collected, to make the coffin function for the deceased and their family. In my first book *The Cost of Death*, I coined the phrase "functional materialism," trying to explain a materiality that created functional mind states like transformation into rebirth after death, or the creation of social capital through display. Tim LeCain argues, "Materiality resides at all scales of human history, not just the macro" (LeCain 2017: 14).

When I have the opportunity to examine a coffin in person, I spend an extraordinary amount of time with that thing, more than some museum staff would like, given the economics of museum space, time, and labor. I crawl about, using a variety of flashlights, photographing and taking notes; muttering to myself, mindful of all kinds of characteristics of the coffin's "objectness" – its materials of wood, plaster, paint, varnish, its craft quality, its craft technique and modifications. Sometimes I have grant money to bring in graduate students or other technical support to help me with photography, digital microscopic analysis, maybe even wood sampling for carbon-14 isotopes to date the wood. All the while, I look for human actions embedded within the object, examining the piece for craft remnants that do not make sense if the piece had been made from scratch for a given coffin owner, things like too many mortis and tenon joins, or two layers of wood modification, or multiple levels of plaster and/or paint decoration. When I examine a coffin I am looking for craft-action – crafting and re-crafting, or otherwise said, reuse.

The fact that most Egyptian coffins were made of wood is essential, as wood comes from living trees, but, even as such, wood, if properly treated, can avoid decay, making it a special commodity for preparation of the dead. Properly treated wood was, in essence, embalmed dead trees. Thus seasoned, the wood could contain a human body also thus preserved. The wood was only one essential part of a coffin though. There were also the resins for those with access to their trade, sap from a living tree or bush created to repel insects in the wild, tapped and collected by humans for the creation of mummies and as a protective coffin varnish.

One also needed animal glues to attach woods as well as plasters, added to the coffins of some time periods to smooth and regularize its surface, forming an even, decorative plane. To this was added pigment – earth matters like red and yellow ochres, huntite or gypsum white, carbon black, yellow and red arsenic, or manufactured matter like blue and green pigments transformed at high heat from natural elements into glass frit to recreate minerals too rare and costly to use on coffins, like lapis lazuli or malachite. Despite a human manufacture one step removed, all the colors in the Egyptian palette were somehow earthbound, and the artisan used them to inscribe the coffin with spells, iconography, and imagery, creating "a sort of coevolutionary process between tools, language, and brains" (LeCain 2017: 121). Each coffin preserves a different signature of materiality, different amounts or types of ingredients negotiated in the competitive arena of access, commission, construction, use, display, and reuse of the piece. Coffins existed within a complicated materialist space in which scarcity was the order of the day. Coffin use did not spring up from the human mind unaided from some abstract notion of Egyptian "religion," whatever that is; Egyptian coffins were a materialist ritual negotiation between the earthly environment and mammalian-human social demands, eventually coalescing into oblong, anthropoid boxes to contain and display the dead.

If a natural disaster sweeps away a town or city or place, we do not say that the storm had no agency. We do not say, when civilization is destroyed, that physical things do not matter (Olsen 2010: 160). By the same token, we cannot place all of the physicality of Egyptian funerary art into the hands of the primary human actor. The coffin was made by people, but its reified existence shaped people thereafter. The thing has some agency over the humanity that created it, informing and constructing the social and the religious. We should understand, as did the Egyptians, that the human condition could not be divorced from the material world of which it was a part. Matter that stopped the decay of dead bodies was scarce in ancient Egypt. It had to be acquired (like resins or cedar or natron), or processed (like Egyptian blue pigment), or constructed (like coffins). These things were not (always) local and freely available. Such resources were unequally acquired and distributed, and, we must assume, controlled by the powerful within a given society. Unlike the oxygen that everyone on our planet has access to, or even water, particularly in Egypt where Nile floodwaters were so plentiful, these crafted coffin objects brought together materiality from near and far – from foreign environments, from the desert, and from blackland Egypt. The antimicrobial and antifungal actions of Arabian frankincense, created in a harsh, arid environment that worked to repel insects, created a highly defensive tree that, once imported into Egypt, could bring protection to a dead body. The characteristics of some wood provided similar powers with antimicrobial affects. On the other hand, palm wood was everywhere in ancient Egypt but made poor coffins.

Tim Le Cain argues, "human ideas emerge from and with the material world around us" (LeCain 2017: 18). Trees are scarce in Egypt. They provide shade, a rarity in a part of the globe where the sun beats down with ferocity. Trees survive on water. These were the same elements thought to be required to recreate and maintain the dead in the afterlife – sun, shade, water. But Egypt – with its continually flooded Nile valley – did not allow the cultivation of enough trees for the elite dead of Egypt to be buried within them. The

Egyptians themselves seem to have been frustrated by the lack of appropriate materials to contain their dead, thus transforming the scarce tree into a social symbol of power par excellence (Arbuckle MacLeod Forthcoming).

Egyptian materiality teaches that "things are not just submissive and plastic beings ready to embody our mental templates or the imperatives of our social wish images" (Olsen 2010: 38). But researchers too often domesticate things by talking about "embodiment" or "exchange" or "discourse," afraid to discuss the wildness and agency of the materiality itself (Olsen 2010: 54). Human beings manipulate objects every day, trying to acquire them, keep them, hoard them, change them, process them, control them, build them, sell them, steal them, recycle them. Anyone who has tried to construct something from scratch knows this – even if it is a simple assembly of manufactured furniture, or a painting, or a loaf of bread. Things have much more control over us than we like. The Egyptian coffin was no different. And thus funerary materiality as a whole was no different.

3 The Egyptian Coffin as a Social Thing

The coffin was just one part of an Egyptian funerary ensemble – including the tomb, with its accessible chapel and sealed, underground burial chamber, sarcophagi, funerary masks, canopic equipment for human organs, *shabti* figurines, underworld papyri, and any number of provisions like bread and beer, furniture and wigs, given to the dead to sustain them in the next life – but the coffin was that burial element closest to the corpse. The coffin named the corpse, represented the corpse, was a forever version of that corpse.

Some objects have a particular staying power, like the furniture in your house that is not gone when you wake up in the morning (Olsen 2010: 158). An Egyptian coffin had a way of maintaining concepts in the ancient Egyptian mind. Once it was deposited into the tomb, the coffin was not present like domestic furniture to be seen and touched every day, but, when another (elite) person in the community died, it was believed essential to procure another such coffin to transform the body and soul, to maintain a physical connection between the living family and the dead ancestor, and to display the wealth and spending ability of the family.

A coffin is just one type of thing in the complex world of ancient Egyptian materiality. Why not focus on the statue? Or the scarab? Or the temple? All are possible subjects to get to the social roots of ancient Egyptian materiality, but the coffin was a different kind of object because it contained dead human flesh and bone at its core, and thus its objectified meaning crossed all kinds of boundaries between this realm and the next, between material and cognition, between belief and ritual. It was part wood, part human; part body, part spirit; part repository of deeply held religious beliefs, part show-off commodity.

There is an unspoken assumption that the ancient Egyptians worked with plenty rather than scarcity and that the materials and craft ability to make a coffin were available to more people than not. I remember my own assumption that coffins were largely available to most Egyptians, not understanding just how much such an object would have cost, let alone three of them in a nesting set. But coffins are key remnants of social inequality, and, as social separators, coffins construct ancient spreadsheets into the varied social lives of ancient peoples. Most people had no access or right to a coffin. Egyptian children generally did not get coffins. When a child was buried in a coffin (and not deposited within a domestic context like underneath the floor of a home), this rarity of funerary spending expressed a clear statement about the unusual social status of that particular child and about the display needs of that particular family (Hayes 1959: 52). Ancient Egyptian elite women had access to coffins just like men, but men benefited more from funerary materiality compared with women (Cooney 2008a, 2010; Meskell 1999) in terms of coffin number and coffin material embellishments. And, as we know, men were more powerful than women in Egyptian society, able to take on professions. Coffins are documents of power.

3.1 Coffins and Social Power

What other social categories could we apply? Foreigners are hard to identify as such in the archaeological record, particularly among the rich and powerful, but studies have been done (Eaton-Krauss et al. 2016; Lakomy 2016; Smith & Buzon 2014b). Non-coffin owners are difficult to find, but Sinuhe did bemoan being buried out of Egypt, wrapped in nothing more than a sheepskin (Lichtheim 1975: 230). Many archaeologists of the past two hundred years have ignored non-coffin owners in a given tomb, due to their lack of crafted materiality, often disposing of such bodies unrecorded and unphotographed. Palm rib mats around a jumble of bones are less exciting and certainly less collectible or displayable compared with coffins containing mummified human remains. Poor burials have not been systematically examined and counted, diminishing any proper comparisons with rich overlords, allowing Egyptologists to call some coffin owners "poor" when they were nothing of the sort, just because our datasets leave so little with which to compare them (Connor 2018; Grajetzki 2003; Smith 1992: 193–231). We are thus left with a material remnant of social power used almost solely by the wealthy, and are driven to examine the entirety of Egyptian society through the lens of the Haves, knowing that the Have Nots were always there under their feet.

Coffins provide all kinds of information about those at the top of society – about time period, social place, spending ability, gender, religious understanding, economic context, trade networks, workshops, education level of the craftsman and, ostensibly, commissioner, ethnic identity if foreign names were inscribed, family connections, all kinds of things. The coffin certainly had a number of religious purposes, the topic over which Egyptology often lingers the most, but this body container also displayed social and economic desires. In other words, ancient Egyptian elites showed off their coffins and other funerary arts hoping to impress their neighbors, friends, and associates, hoping to broadcast a certain social reality for a few days of display in this world and for all the days after in the next. This would certainly be a natural human thing to desire, something people still do today at public events like weddings, the display potential of which is circumscribed and must be maximized to greatest effect. If one cannot afford a wedding, for example, then the entire display might be scrapped, choosing a bureaucratic courtroom affair instead. If family members cannot afford the price of a public funeral today, then a loved one is disposed of with no one watching in a pauper's cremation. If you cannot pay for display, then you get limited materiality.

3.2 Coffins and Social Display

To study objects is to resurrect social power itself. This is not to say we are only examining what the coffin "embodies" in terms of religious or ritual or social meaning, but that we are studying the coffin as an almost living and breathing remnant of elite social life, thus harnessing the object nature of the piece and reverse engineering the social and economic and ritual processes that went into it.

As such, the coffin has powerful social memories for Arabic-speaking Egyptians even today. There is a phrase still spoken amongst traditional Egyptian village and city dwellers, particularly the older members of those communities: جهاز البنت كفنها, *Gehaz el bint kafanha*, "The furniture (or 'pride') of the girl is her coffin."[1] Comparing the betrothal furniture with the coffin she receives at her death is to remark upon its social value, its display potential, a social marker that lasts with a family, something that confers pride and separates those who participate in scarce materiality from the vast majority who can only afford the barest of provisions. Those individuals in village society who have no funds for betrothal furniture would likely also not get an

---

[1] Fadel Gad and Amr Shahat, personal communication, 2019.

ostentatious celebration at their death – because when there is no wedding, there is often no funeral. In short: the lack of the money for the thing translates into the inability to construct social display possibilities.

And so, the social power of the coffin continues to maintain its wedge-like social meaning in Egyptian modern society – even when coffins and tombs do not have the power they once did in largely Muslim religious contexts that now specifically speak against elaboration of bodies or funerary goods or spaces. But so powerful was the materialization of Egyptian social differences through funerary objects like coffins and papyri and tombs, that when the dead are buried today in Egypt in provincial places, particularly in Upper Egypt, a special *sheikh* is brought in when the dirt is placed over the body to recite the Talkeen el Mayet تلقين الميت, a long list of things the deceased will need to say when they arrive at certain gates.[2] Specific demons are described; the questions and required answers are chanted in the ritual. This ritual is not found in the Koran or the Hadith, but is a remnant of ancient Egyptian social practice, once preserved on papyri and tomb walls for the wealthy and now imparted verbally to the dead when their families can access (and pay) the special *sheikh* who knows the ritual. There are no Egyptian-like objects to encode such belief systems at funerals today – no underworld books or maps, none of the coffins with names and inscriptions – but the understanding continues that some people will benefit from the social ability to procure special knowledge for the afterlife and some will not. The rite exemplifies the sustained power of previous religious materiality.

People purchase special access and displays all the time to reify social differences vis-à-vis one another. At the Egyptian funeral, the coffin set was key, representing an enormous investment of time, money, and energy that went into the production of the entire funerary ensemble. At the modern Western wedding, the bridal gown is a key object, and, like the coffin, it is also displayed publicly in a short-term, highly visible setting. The modern wedding also includes other objects, like rings, that participants display for a longer period of time beyond the ceremony and use afterwards as heirlooms – like the ancient Egyptian tomb chapel, which could be visited on feast days for generations after the patriarch's funeral. In today's wedding preparations, the gown and ring draw the most energy and expense.[3] Venue is also important for the wedding, as this

---

[2] Fadel Gad and Amr Shahat, personal communication, 2019.

[3] For a study of average costs of the American wedding in 2018, see Editor 2019, This is What American Weddings Look Like Today, *Brides* [Online], www.brides.com/gallery/american-wedding-study [accessed September 21, 2019]. In this study, we learn that the average cost of the wedding increased from .$27,000 in 2017 to $47,000 in 2018, that an average of 167 people were invited to the American wedding, that the cost of most weddings was borne by the parents of the bride and groom, and that the cost of the dress increased from $1,562 in 2017 to $2,260 in

determines visibility, the time allowed to display the procured objects, and the number of people to which one can display. All of these expenses are negotiated by the relevant parties. Think how much arguing there is amongst family members about where the wedding will be, what the dress will look like, how big a diamond can be purchased or if a family heirloom will be gifted, and who will be invited. Weddings are socially negotiated events. The stakes are high. A tacky or cheap wedding translates into an unworthy family. Scarcity haunts all negotiations; every family must decide where to spend funds and where to cut back. There is almost always someone in the family willing to go overboard, even driving the family into debt, to create the biggest social impact possible, just as there is always someone hyper-thrifty hoping not to spend anything, pulling back resources even for reasonable things.

We must try to imagine the Egyptian funeral, of which the coffin is a remnant, as a rite of great expense that demanded family negotiation within a context of socially negotiated scarcity. The objects involved in the funerary rituals are the remnants of the display, but they are also social depositories of an elite family's power. The economic context must be taken into account to understand what level of scarcity people were confronting. Indeed, most of the Egyptian coffins discussed in this Element find their origin within a time when economic growth was stagnant or on a steep downward slide. Funerary assemblages from contexts of crisis were not intensified or embellished, but rather condensed and constricted, limiting the typical funerary ensemble of a typical elite person to a nesting coffin set, a few papyri, ushabti and canopic equipment, and a few other objects. The 18th Dynasty tomb stuffed full of daily-life wealth – dozens of sheets and blankets, wigs and perfumes, stacks of clothing – was a thing of the past. Even the 19th Dynasty decorated and accessible tomb chapel was dispensed with as the 20th Dynasty continued, as it marked tombs' best-kept secret during times of graveyard insecurity.

For those who could afford it, the coffin was the main avenue to a particular kind of afterlife. The Egyptian coffin was a container for a dead body, but its religious function was by no means simple. A coffin was thought to act as a kind of transformative device that turned the deceased into an eternal god-like form, meaning that, for the ancient Egyptians, the coffin was nothing less than a magical object able to make the dead come alive and communicate with the

2018. For the cost of rings and flowers (engagement rings cost on average $7,829 and flowers $2,629), see Park 2019, Here's How Much the Average Wedding in 2018 Cost – and Who Paid, *Brides* [Online], www.brides.com/story/american-wedding-study-how-much-average-wedding-2018-cost. The survey represents a middle-class segment of the population for whom weddings were attainable, much as ancient Egyptian coffin prices represent only those for whom disposable income could be spent on coffins.

living. These supernatural powers might cause us to discount the coffin's function as a marker of social place – of gender, of position, and of wealth. But the coffin was placed at the center of every funerary procession and ritual, meaning that every member of the audience looked to it for social markers, like gold, expensive blue and green paints, and painstaking craftsmanship.

The coffin was a product of its society and audience members were likely not reading religious texts as the coffin went by in procession. They were commenting on style and materials and choice. Style changes, in and of themselves, suggest that the ancient Egyptians competed with one another for the most fashionable coffins. Fashion was by no means restricted to visual style and not mutually exclusive to religious activities or archaism. Ancient Egyptian ritual objects, like coffins, were at the vortex of practical religious beliefs within a social arena.

In this Element, we will focus on the entire "lifespan" of the coffin – how they were created, who bought them, how they were used in funerary rituals, where they were placed in a given tomb, and how they might have been used again for another dead person. We will move through time from the initial agreement between the craftsman and the seller, to the construction of the object by a carpenter, to the plastering and painting of the coffin by a draftsman, to the sale of the object, to its ritual use in funerary activities, to its deposit in a burial chamber, and, briefly, to its possible reuse (Cooney Forthcoming-b).

To examine the Egyptian coffin in such detail, we need to focus on one particular time period – 1295 to 945 BCE – not because it was a high point of coffin production necessarily, but because this particular slice of time provides a mass of information about craft specialization, economic exchanges, and social change. Egyptologists characterize the roughly 300 years from 1295 to 1070 BCE as the second half of the New Kingdom, also known as the "Ramesside Period," which began with Ramses I and ended with Ramses XI. The Ramesside Period is composed of two dynasties: the 19th Dynasty, during which Egypt's hegemony in Canaan and Nubia was expanded and defended by kings like Seti I and Ramses II, and the 20th Dynasty when political and economic systems broke down, resulting in a splintered and impoverished Egypt (Cooney Forthcoming-a). The years 1070 to 945 BCE mark the transition from the Bronze Age to the Iron Age and make up the first part of the Third Intermediate Period, comprising Dynasties 21 and early 22 when the rule of the Egyptian king was restricted to the Delta, while rule of the south was taken over by the Amen Priesthood. The cause of the Bronze Age Collapse is much discussed, but a series of events marked the 20th Dynasty as a time of rapid, transformative, and unavoidable change (Bryce 2003, 2009; Cline 1994, 2014; Cline & O'Connor 2012; Drews 1995; Emanuel 2017; Iacono 2019; Knapp &

Manning 2016; Kramer-Hajos 2016; Murray 2017; Pfoh 2016; Yasur-Landau 2010).

Thus we are focusing on this slice of time between 1295 to 945 BCE because it was characterized by extraordinary preservation, albeit uneven, in coffin and text materiality as well as diachronic social change. In many ways, this is the *only* time from ancient Egypt for which there is enough information to tell a detailed story about the social meaning and use of the Egyptian coffin, because we can most clearly see how the object demanded adaptation and negotiation. Most of the written documentation about coffin production and use comes from the Ramesside Period, while most of the object documentation, in the form of coffins, comes from the Third Intermediate Period thereafter. We thus have skewed datasets in which there are low numbers of coffins surviving from the 19th and 20th Dynasties, fewer than 100 in total, including all fragments, but for which we have the most detailed economic evidence in terms of prices and workshops. Dynasties 21 and 22, on the other hand, preserve almost no texts about the economics of funerary production and yet a massive number of coffins, as many as 1,000 in total, can be examined.

4 The Object as Container of Transformative Magic

Egyptologists really only know about the funerary ceremonies of the wealthy because these were the people who had the privilege of commissioning painted tombs, illuminated books of the dead, carved sarcophagi, and painted coffins, all of which left material traces of the funeral's form and practice in the archaeological record. All of the evidence points to the Opening of the Mouth ritual as the key moment of the funeral, in which a priest held a variety of implements to the "active" parts (eyes, ears, nose, inscribed name, etc.) of an object to enliven it (Assmann 2005). Opening of the Mouth rites may have been performed on a number of different objects associated with the deceased – the mummy, coffin, sarcophagus, and statuary – so that each could be awakened and empowered to act as a vessel for the soul of the dead. But the coffin was always at the center of the funeral, that first and last barrier between the profane world and the mummified corpse. The coffin was thus covered with magical incantations and spells from the Book of the Dead, images of deities who exercised great power in the netherworld (Quirke 2013).

The coffin was so powerful that most wealthy individuals demanded a coffin *set* made up of multiple coffins, wishing to surround their mummy with more than one layer of protection. In the New Kingdom, multiple human-shaped coffins fit inside one another, nesting like Russian dolls, each layer in a set adding another magical force field that shielded the vulnerable dead from the many destructive forces in the netherworld.

It is easy in our time of quick and cheap materiality to forget just how expensive handcrafted wooden coffins were. Indeed, data indicates that many elites could not afford a set with three full coffins, instead using nesting coffins and a mummy board, the latter a long cover that lay over the body, a kind of "cheat" coffin. To this might be added a mummy mask that fitted over the head and upper chest. Only the most wealthy could afford to place their coffins into stone or wooden outer sarcophagi, providing a fourth or fifth layer of protection. The set of Tutankhamun – the 18th Dynasty king whose tomb was found intact by Howard Carter – included three coffins, one mummy mask, one stone sarcophagus, and four outer gilded shrines, resulting in nine layers of protection. For the ancient Egyptians, nine was a magical number. Nine was 3 x 3, plurality times plurality; in other words, infinite protection (Velde 1971). We have no other intact New Kingdom royal burial, but this high number of coffins may have been reserved for royalty. Wealthy Egyptians made do with different permutations of one, two, or three coffins, and maybe additional pieces like mummy masks, mummy boards, or stone sarcophagi. When crisis and scarcity struck in the 20th Dynasty, the Egyptians began to standardize the elite coffin set to two nesting coffins plus a mummy board.

The typical Ramesside coffin was "anthropoid," which means the coffin had roughly the shape of the human body – with a carved head and chest and sometimes modeled legs, arms, and feet. Essentially, the coffin was a wooden body replacement (or body improvement) for the deceased – one that could act eternally as a vessel for the soul as it came and went from the underworld. Nineteenth to 21st Dynasty coffins are almost always yellow – the color of the sun god Re. If you were a rich person, then that yellow color was provided by thinly hammered and etched gold attached to the wood. If you were reasonably wealthy, then you had a pistacia resin varnish painted over a white, or maybe a sparkly yellow orpiment pigment mixed with yellow ochre, background, providing a lustrous yellow. If you were lucky to scrape together the funds to buy one coffin, you probably used cheap yellow ochre paint to give your flesh the color of the sun god. Before the Ramesside Period, coffins of mid- to late 18th Dynasty were black, either painted with carbon black paint or the more costly variation, a tar-like black varnish that reflected light, likening the deceased to Osiris and the fertile land of Egypt melded with the sun god. Fashions changed, however, and solarizing yellow coffins ruled from the end of the 18th Dynasty, around 1300 BCE, to the very beginning of the 22nd Dynasty, around 900 BCE.

The case sides of 19th-Dynasty coffins were formulaic and regular – each side decorated with two of the four Sons of Horus, Thoth, Anubis, and a great deal of text from chapters 151 and 161 from the Book of the Dead, including words spoken by these gods in protection of the deceased inside the coffin (Lüscher 1998). The 21st-Dynasty coffin case sides were different, including a much wider variety of scenes from the Book of the Dead and other more secret funerary iconography – the deceased standing before Osiris, Hathor emerging from the Western mountains, the deceased standing before the tribunal during the weighing of his heart, even esoteric images of solar-Osirian unification like Sokar coming out of a pyramidal hill (Broekman et al. 2018; Manassa & Darnell 2004; Niwiński 1988). Something happened in the later Ramesside Period that allowed people more leeway in their choice of coffin design. Artisans and commissioners moved toward densely painted exteriors and decorated coffin interiors too, which had previously only been painted with thick black varnish. The difference between the 19th and 20th Dynasty coffins are so dramatic they cause us to wonder *how* and *why* such stylistic changes happened when they happened. Interestingly, these style changes coincided with the first coffin reuse. Were people using the new and busy coffin decoration to cover over older decoration? A complicated polychrome design covered a multitude of sins. Or perhaps coffin buyers were worried that the old-style coffins were not providing the dead with what they needed from a religious perspective. Maybe fashions were motivated by anxious commissioners who could not have decorated tomb chapels, statuary, and other highly visible tomb goods.

4.1 The Coffin as a Microcosm of the Universe

When the deceased was placed inside the coffin at the funerary ceremonies, they were placed inside the sky goddess Nut, inside the womb of a mother figure, to create a regenerated identity (Taylor 2001, 2010). But the Egyptians also believed that inside the sky was a netherworld space – full of both frightening demons and regenerative powers. This they called the *duat*, "all that is not land or sky," the realm of the dead, the entrance of which was beneath the western horizon, even beneath the earth in some cases. The *duat* space continued within the sky, within the body of the goddess Nut high up into the heavens (Allen 1988).

If you look at a New Kingdom coffin in a museum, you will see the *duat* depicted in a frightening and evocative way. The coffin interior was almost always painted with a thick, black varnish, giving the appearance of a massive void (Cooney 2007). You can imagine the emotions of family members when the body was placed into this blackness at the funeral. It was frightening, yes, but it was also a reminder that the dead person was going to the *duat*, to a womb where regeneration was possible. Later in the 21st Dynasty, the Egyptians became more figural in their understanding of this space when they painted the coffin interior with images of the gods that inhabited it.

In fact, the anthropoid coffin as a whole can be seen as a representation of a future state of being for the dead. The dead man or woman was shown awake, eyes open, mouth often smiling, hands engaged and sometimes grasping protective symbols. This image must have been comforting to the grieving family members. On the one hand, the dead person was shown as they would have been in the funeral, covered with flower garlands, with potential for rebirth and transformation. On the other hand, the dead individual was depicted awake and alert, wearing a formal wig and sometimes jewelry and a pure white garment, as if they had already been transformed into one of the Blessed Dead who would never suffer what the Egyptians feared most: a second death (Assmann 2005). For these ancient people the coffin was a kind of cocoon (Bettum 2011), but it was also a representation of a deified deceased. The *inside* of the coffin could be understood differently from the external depiction on the *outside* coffin lid. In other words, the coffin represents both the mechanism for rebirth (the contained female space) at the same time that it depicted the individual to be transformed (the preserved corpse wrapped in the manner of the masculine god Osiris).

It is also possible to see the coffin as a mini temple for the deceased (Van Walsem 1997). The dead individual was represented receiving offerings from their family, being led into the company of the gods, and in worship of the gods. The dead person was identified as "true of voice," thus predestined for a good afterlife, and called "venerated" in the numerous hieroglyphic texts. The coffin itself represented the dead person as an Osiris-like being, arms bound across the chest, body bound into a mummiform shape – the state of the dead at the funeral. But the two-dimensional drawings of the dead man or woman on the coffin lid show them as a fully transformed member of the Blessed Dead after their transformation – wearing pure white, with a scented fat cone on their head, with a fully articulated human body, and with their own male or female identity. The coffin itself showed the deceased as they needed to be at their transformation – as an Osiris worthy of worship – but the depictions on the coffin represented what the deceased was to become – one of the Blessed Dead – as a fait accompli.

The Egyptian coffin was a home, a fortress, a tomb, a temple, and even a magical provisioning device for food, water, clothing, and incense. And when it was placed in the burial chamber, it could provide the deceased with a map of the underworld. By being placed in the tomb properly, the dead would know which way was west, allowing them to enter the *duat* for their transformation. The coffin provided these powers by means of a *material object* of wood, plaster, and paint. To make a material transformation, one needed a magical material tool. The coffin was that tool.

5 The Coffin as a Set of Social and Economic Choices

Many Egyptologists become so wrapped up in religious meaning – of coffins, temples, inscriptions – that it seems everything in ancient Egypt was religiously determined, that religious belief itself led all style choices in coffin design. Because of the coffin's overwhelming and obvious religious importance, it is easy to forget the social implications of funerary arts purchases. It is easy to overlook that all of these funerary objects cost something; that funerary objects were expensive; that not everyone was able to afford the same things or did not want the same things. As Olsen argues, "Embodiment becomes a process of materialization whereby selfhood, gender, cosmological entities, and so on are imbued in matter" (Olsen 2010).

Scarcity affected all, even the king. Lacking limitless resources, coffins demanded choices by the people who ordered them. Even wealthy people had to sacrifice something to buy coffins. For the rich, coffin embellishments might have translated into cutting back on comforts within the home, like not buying another set of finely woven linen sheets, or not investing in more sheep and goats that year. If mid-level elites or skilled artisans wanted to save money for multi-piece coffin sets, they would have had to make harder choices than high elites, taking in more weaving orders, maybe pulling a child's education and putting them to work, selling more animals from the family herd, or the time of their cleaning girl, or a parcel of land meant for their daughter's dowry – all in order to buy coffins and funerary equipment. No one could afford whatever they wanted; everyone had to make choices based on their budget. And we should assume that not everyone in a given family unit always agreed on what was most important in a coffin set.

First we can ask: what are the components of the Egyptian coffin production system? These might include 1) demand for coffins (how many people could actually commission and buy them), 2) the availability of artisanal skill and the reputational capital of those artisans, 3) the means of production, including wood, plaster, paints, varnish, and the organizational workshop resources such as space to work, a means to work, including proper tools, lighting, and optimum conditions, and 4) distribution (how far a given workshop could reach coffin buyers demanding product). All of these components affect the output of the product. If elites were suddenly without the means to purchase, it did not matter that they had access to meticulously trained state craftsmen. If access to resins was compromised, people might have to forgo varnish or find substandard alternatives. If a craftsman misplaced an important and expensive tool, he would not be able to work, no matter how skilled he was, until he replaced it. If high-level artisans were not available for elite commissions for whatever reason, elites might have had to travel farther to find coffin creation that met their social standards, or they might have decided to go with a lesser artisan.

Adding to this, there were other variables that affected coffin output, in particular social stability, which also determined graveyard security. If Egyptian society was in crisis, experiencing sudden change, detrimentally affecting elite connections to one another, or elite connections to their king, high priest, or other patron, then coffin demand and production could be adversely affected. If Egyptian society was thriving, with all patronage relationships functioning well, then this would affect coffin demand and production positively, resulting in the hiring and training of more artisans, the consumption of more capital, and an increase in trade and mineral acquisition. High demand would likely also result in the increased specialization of artisans, some denoted as specifically doing carpentry, others with titles connoting draftsmanship. Lower demand for elite craft goods would translate into craftsmen making do with narrow specializations, working on a variety of craftwork, and becoming jacks-of-all-trades. A lack of specialization could mark institutional abandonment of investment in craftwork. The more specialized a craftsman was, the more institutionally complex a given system was.

The strength of larger institutions – like the king and his vizierate, or the High Priesthood of Amun – was another variable in coffin crafting, as weakness in royal monopolies of trade or mining or workshop support could throw all kinds of wrenches into the works.

Finally, religious beliefs and ritual demands were additional variables that affected coffin production; things needed to be done in certain, traditional ways so that the magic was believed functional by purchasers. Deep religious beliefs might have caused people to adapt quickly if faced with problems in coffin production – because if you thought your loved one might be denied an afterlife without the right funerary materiality, you would do all kinds of things previously thought immoral to get that materiality, including coffin reuse.

All of these variables allowed substitutions and adaptations (Rondano 2020). Just as one artisan could take the place of another who was sick or unable to work, so too could cartonnage be substituted for wood, or a limited color palette for a richer palette including manufactured blue and green pigments. Yellow paint could be used instead of varnish; varnish could be substituted for gold.

One patron of craft installations could be substituted for another if a given institution was not functioning. One source of natron could be substituted for another if compromised. One ritual could substitute for another if choice of coffin text spells or Book of the Dead chapters are any indication (Allen 2006; Scalf 2017). Even beliefs in what was right and wrong, efficacious or non-functional, could be substituted, in that coffins made from scratch could be substituted with reused coffins.

5.1 Coffins and Craft Culture

In many ways, it is useful to think of coffin creation in the Ramesside and Third Intermediate Periods (Cooney 2007, 2011; Jørgensen 2001; Niwiński 1987; Raven 2017; Taylor 1985) as craft culture, as communities of practice, rather than a series of workshops (Costin & Wright 1998; Wenger 1998). Craft culture was a flexible and malleable system with many moving parts within a complicated and changing society, with many variables intersecting and influencing one another. People and systems, things and resources, were all pulled together to meet social and religious demands for elite social display and religious transformation through funerary goods.

Sometimes institutional patrons were essential and there is evidence that the crown could bestow a gift of red granite from their quarry monopoly, for instance, to a grateful official, or a plot of land in the necropolis for a family tomb. But at other times, those institutional patrons had less to give, demanding privatization as institutional funding was pulled – from craft installations, material procurement, specialization in ritual and religious work, even temple building and upkeep. Privatization demanded capital and flexibility from elites interested in procuring funerary goods; thus when even the state resources failed to provide the burial plot, guards for the burial grounds, trade networks for wood materials, and the support of craft installations, people got innovative. They cultivated and used native woods; they reused coffins they owned within their family tombs, sometimes generationally, like the coffin of Tabekhnet, reused by her daughter Nany, according to the genealogy provided on their shared Book of the Dead papyrus (MMA 30.3.31); they made do with different materials, simpler rituals, craftsmen with less reputational value. They created a market for looted or abandoned funerary goods. People were less reliant on government institutions in ancient Egypt if they had to be. Examination of funerary behavior during a time of crisis and scarcity is incredibly useful, because it reduces what was thought necessary to the lowest common denominators, and one recognizes not only adaptations, but also the minimum necessary to maintain social power in a functional ancient Egyptian community.

The coffins preserved to us are remnants of social negotiations and an attempt is made here to follow the cautions of David Wengrow that there has been a "tendency to assume that all categories of grave goods act to dignify individuation and wealth in the same way, such that every kind of material deposit, from a lapis lazuli necklace to a sacrificed animal, can be arranged on a single scale of value and used to index the status of the deceased" (Wengrow 2006: 73). Thus, coffins should best be compared with other coffins, and not every group of ancient Egyptians valued coffins in the same way, but rather as "new interest groups in search of ways to reproduce their own identities and expand their functions within society" (Wengrow 2006: 218). Some groups favored the quantity of expensive materials over the quality of draftsmanship; other groups had more appreciation for careful and meticulous painting. The coffins reveal that social milieu conditioned tastes and values of everything, even involving the purchase of one of the most religiously charged objects imaginable.

It seems obvious that different people with different social contexts would demand different coffins – even while they shared the same general religious beliefs, culture, language, and government (Bourdieu 1984). However, synthetic research might create the assumption that most ancient Egyptians wanted the same elements in their funerary arts; that their religious activities were more or less the same at one moment in time; that their understanding of funerary arts' utility and function was more homogenous; that the elite condition was the universal Egyptian condition (Assmann 2005). To the outsider, funerary arts all look the same, after all, but heterogeneity is there nonetheless. The differences in style and content may be nuanced, slight, and overlooked by the uninitiated, but they are as clear as day for those immersed in the materiality.

Coffins are religious objects containing a corpse, but let us artificially extract them from their highly charged ritual environment and place them into an arena of social competition. If we treat ancient society monolithically, Egyptian or otherwise, it is easy to assume that there was an ideal Egyptian coffin somewhere out there in the world, a Coffin with a capital C, so to speak, and that every ancient Egyptian felt the same way about this ideal coffin, that it was thought to perform the same perfected functions by everyone who saw it. But if we notice that not everyone could afford said ideal coffin, and thus had to make do without certain aspects of it, this would explain why different tastes and fashions developed in coffin style, material, and text. On the most simple level: some coffins cost a great deal of money, others only a little. That much is easily seen in the prices preserved in west Theban texts, but close examination of the coffins preserved in museums around the world shows the same variability, because some are fully gilded and others barely painted. Some have lots of functional hieroglyphic text, others barely any. Coffin materials, styles, tastes, and values depended on the embedded social context of the maker, buyer, user, and consumer.

Indeed, two different coffins with the same price range might have looked radically different. Different social groups made different social choices about their funerary arts. I have defined four different social groups amongst Ramesside (19th and 20th Dynasty) coffins: 1) a high elite group, 2) a medium-level elite group, 3) an artisan group, and 4) a lower-level social group that could barely scrape together the resources for a coffin. Coffins of the 21st Dynasty show a similar distribution (Cooney Forthcoming-b). Each group had different spending abilities, yes, but, in addition, each group had a different set of aesthetic sensibilities – tastes defined by their social milieu for their social milieu and reinforced by the materiality itself. Since most of these coffins come from Thebes originally, we can rule out many, but not all, regional variations.

The coffin set of Ta-Kayt (Cooney 2007: 407; Bayer-Niemeier et al. 1993: 302–23; Geßler-Löhr 1981: 25–7; Niwiński 1988: 140) (Figure 5) probably belonged to a medium-level female elite – group 2 – people not from the highest echelons of society but who wanted or needed to show their more limited wealth in the most ostentatious way possible, focusing on expensive Egyptian blue pigment at the expense of careful draftsmanship. The rough painting application on the coffins' collars is testament to this. Ta-kayt's coffins came to the Liegieghaus Museum in Frankfurt in the nineteenth century as an art market purchase. Ta-kayt was a chantress of Amen and that Theban title was inscribed on her coffin. Her temple association was a social advantage as much as it was religious capital to use in the afterlife. In other words, this temple position provided her and other women like her with social prestige and status in addition to religious participation in a sacred cult. And while "Chantress of Amen" could connote a very high position for some women, Ta-kayt's coffins make it pretty clear that neither she nor her family moved in the highest circles of society. She was probably married to a mid-level elite priest or was part of a mid-level elite priestly family in Thebes. How do we know this? Have any other documents about Ta-kayt been preserved? No. We only have comparative visual analysis of her preserved materiality.

Indeed, the circumstances of this coffin set's creation, as like all the others, are unknown. We do not know how Ta-kayt's coffins were commissioned – if the lady made the choices herself long before her death, or if family leaders took the decision-making role from her because of her gender. The text information from western Thebes about other coffin orders suggests that women may have bought funerary arts on their own, ordering their coffins in advance of death. It was certainly in Ta-kayt's best interest to have the objects all worked out in advance, but we will never know the details of her funerary planning. Egyptian

Figure 5 Coffin set of Ta-kayt, 19th Dynasty, Liegieghaus Museum, Frankfurt, 1651a–f.

coffins do not come with their original receipts telling us how much they cost and who purchased them. There are a number of ancient coffin receipts preserved to us, but they do not refer to objects that survive (but cf. Van Walsem 2000).

We do know that Ta-kayt owned at least four pieces in her coffin set: an outer anthropoid coffin, an inner anthropoid coffin, a mummy mask, and a lower mummy board. Based on intact burials of the Ramesside Period, it is possible that all of these nesting funerary objects were placed inside an additional piece that did not survive, a large rectangular sarcophagus, made of wood or even limestone, but probably not granite or granodiorite. These funerary objects betray aesthetic tastes and economic choices made by Ta-kayt's social group that exclude her from a high-elite society that could acquire granite. If you glance at the coffins of Ta-kayt in Frankfurt, you notice almost immediately that the draftsman decided to use thickly applied blue paint for the vast majority of figural designs and hieroglyphic texts. Only in some scenes did he pick out details in white, red, black, or green paint. When he did, it was always on the coffin lid, where the most attention would have been paid by the audience in the Opening of the Mouth ceremonies and other funerary rites.

In fact, the first impression one gets when viewing this coffin set in Frankfurt might be "it is all blue," which was probably *exactly* what the family and deceased lady wanted an audience member of the funerary cortège to think. Egyptian blue paint was made from ground glass frit, and, as a multi-step, high-fired product, it was an expensive pigment, certainly more expensive than red ochre, yellow ochre, black carbon, or white gypsum, substances which were all more readily available in nature. Blue was similar in cost to green pigment, which was also made from a ground frit (Cooney 2007: 213–18). And that was not all: the background of this coffin was painted with another high cost pigment – yellow orpiment – which, despite some overzealous museum restoration in the early twentieth century, is still sparkly and bright in hue. This pigment screamed its value to consuming Egyptian eyes. Orpiment was costly; pure orpiment paint has only been found on objects of royalty (Takahashi et al. 2013). When the elites used it, it seems they layered orpiment with yellow ochre because of the expense. (Cooney 2007: 407–12).

So, we see some nice materials on the coffin set of Ta-kayt. What else? If you look closer at this coffin set, you will notice that the draftsmanship lacks precision. The lines are all of medium width; there is no fine-lined detail. There is very little polychromy. Even though the draftsman was painting almost exclusively in expensive yellow orpiment wash and Egyptian blue, the figures were quickly and unevenly drawn. The case sides look almost like an afterthought. All of this betrays the fact that Ta-kayt belonged to a social group that valued fine materials over fine craftsmanship. Or maybe this social group did not even *understand* the value of high quality painting or carpentry, not having been exposed to it enough in their circles, not being embedded in that community of practice. Whatever the reasons, whoever ordered this coffin appreciated expensive materials over careful craftsmanship. It is likely the draftsman who did this work knew the lower appreciation of his clients for draftsmanship. His line is assured, suggesting that he could probably have done a better job if he had wanted to. Instead, it is likely that the draftsman knew he did not *need* to, because the clients from this social group just did not care or would not notice.

The materials on Ta-kayt's coffin even included some gold foil on the faces and hands of the inner pieces in the set, giving her the flesh of the gods in material form. The commissioners could not afford to gild all the coffin pieces.

Indeed, gold was not placed on Ta-kayt's outer coffin at all, and this might also indicate that most of the audience's attention during these funerary rituals was meant to be paid to the inner pieces in the set that *were* gilded, because it is on these pieces that we also see glass inlay and other time-consuming techniques like raised plaster relief work. Choices had to be made, it seems, and if the social group of Ta-kayt spent the money, they put it where people were looking. Less visible parts of the coffin were virtually ignored, covered with quickly applied blue figures. This is not the only Ramesside coffin set that betrays these tastes and values. There is another such set in the Louvre belonging to a woman named Ta-mut-nofret, and another in the British Museum belonging to a woman named Ka-tebet. And for the 21st Dynasty, there are numerous coffins in the Bab el Gasus cache in which draftsmanship is lacking, but high-quality materials like varnish and pigment are highlighted on the coffin lid.

5.2 Coffins and the Egyptian Funeral

Extending our experiment of seeing the coffin primarily through a socioeconomic lens, let us compare the ancient Egyptian funeral, with the coffin at the center, with the American wedding, with the bridal dress at the center. Although the bridal display does not approach the religious meaning of the coffin, both ceremonies are ideological in nature. Though a wedding is ostensibly joyful and the funeral somber, making this an imperfect comparison, the analogy allows us to understand the habitus of social groups within more familiar surroundings. Our first hypothetical wedding takes place in a Hyatt hotel in Houston, Texas, with a guest list of 200 people. The bride wears a fashionable dress from Nordstrom's bridal collection crafted with yards of silk-satin, priced in the low five figures, with a new diamond necklace, a carefully coiffed up-do with an additional hair-fall to fill out the height, and a rented diamond tiara with a retail price in the high six figures. Hair and makeup make the bride look quite different from her normal self; this is a special day after all, a day to differentiate oneself, to go all-out. Everyone has already seen and admired her two-carat engagement ring, so that expense goes without saying. The family of this particular bride comes from an upper-middle-class social group (father is a surgeon, mother is a homemaker) that values showing off cash outlay by putting it into the most obvious parts of the wedding ceremony, communicating with an audience that (for the most part) shares their tastes and values. In this wedding, the groom's attire is a rented formal morning coat in grey and it is somewhat ill-fitting. At this particular wedding, it is safe to say that more was spent on the bride's undergarments (also displayed before the ceremony to a more intimate selection of bridal attendants, and then presumably to her husband later), than on the groom's attire. A wedding is not a funeral, to be sure, but the analogy works because both events revolve around ritual, social display, important rites of passage, and both occur within embedded communities of practice.

The Egyptian funeral was a complicated ritual procedure and thus a place of similar social and economic exhibition. Ta-kayt put most of her visible wealth onto the head and chest of the innermost pieces, where the most intricate of the Opening of the Mouth rites were performed and to which people's attention would be drawn as priests activated the mouth, eyes, ears, nose, and hands of the dead person.

Many of the coffin prices from west Theban texts corroborate such spending practices. In many such prices, the smaller piece in a given coffin set was much more expensive than the larger (Cooney 2007: 99–100), likely because buyers placed a limited amount of high-cost materials on smaller pieces, making their price much higher than even the larger outer coffin which had no such embellishments.

In other words, when we examine ancient Egyptian coffins closely, ancient choice-making can be reconstructed: if I only have this much money, how do I spend it? How would my friends and colleagues, the people that I most want to impress, spend their funerary arts money and can I do better? This is one way that the coffin materiality controls the buyer, boxing them in, demanding choice-making within a reality of limited economic ability and social habitus.

So what about the highest elites and their larger budgets? One coffin set, now in the British Museum, belonging to a woman named Henutmehyt, betrays high-status social and economic sensibilities (Taylor 1999), (Figure 6a, b, and c). Like Ta-kayt, Henutmehyt also lived in Thebes during the 19th Dynasty. Like Ta-kayt, she had the same title inscribed on her coffin – Chantress of Amen. Like Ta-kayt, she owned an outer coffin, an inner coffin, a mummy mask, and a mummy board, made of wood, plastered and painted, with embellishment in gold and glass inlay. But a quick comparison between the coffin set in Frankfurt and the set in London betrays the differences in social status, taste, and understanding between the two women, and reveals more about the two social groups of which each woman was a part.

Henutmehyt belonged to group 1. Her inner coffin, mummy mask, and lower mummy board are all gilded on the outer surfaces. Henutmehyt owned an outer coffin that was not fully gilded, but it had both gilded face and hands and, more importantly, it was made of imported cedar from the Lebanon. The lack of gilding here may have allowed intimate associates to see the wood grain under the polychromy (or perhaps family members subtly spread the word about the precious wood themselves). Henutmehyt's social group reveled in showing

(a)   (b)   (c)

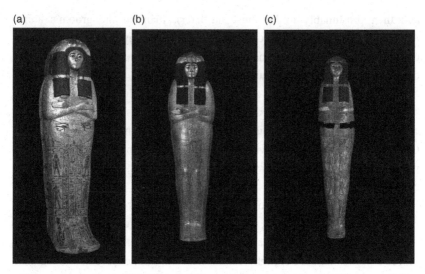

Figure 6a, b, and c Coffin set of Henutmehyt, probably 19th Dynasty, EA 48001, 51001 © Trustees of the British Museum.

great wealth within a closed society of few, and not to the masses. Her outer coffin is actually the only Ramesside coffin known to be made of this expensive wood. The cedar represents a perplexing use of wealth because wood type was not very visible in a plastered and painted polychrome coffin – except perhaps to the most cultivated (or informed) audiences. Henutmehyt's outer coffin displays carefully painted polychrome scenes and texts, with added fine-lined details. There is a good deal of blue paint, but not at the expense of the rest of the polychrome decoration. Thus the labor of the ostensibly reputable craftsman – to dip in and out of a palette of colors – was considered more valuable than a preponderance of expensive Egyptian blue pigment.

The craftsmen who made Henutmehyt's coffin gave attention to all coffin parts even though they would not be a focus in the Opening of the Mouth rituals, carefully painting the bottom of the feet and the case sides, which only a perceptive and shrewd crowd would notice. Perhaps purchasers in this social group made craft choices on the defensive, knowing that rivals would actually be *looking* for oversights upon which to comment. The glass inlay and open-work carving with its beveled edges were completed with skill and careful symmetry. Henutmehyt's social group understood that they needed to link expensive materials with masterful craftsmanship for an audience of sophisticated, educated, critical elites with a highly tuned visual vocabulary, looking to nitpick the coffins of their friends, family, and colleagues. This was *their* community of practice.

Now might be a good time to return to our wedding analogy. Imagine a high-class affair taking place at the Pierre Hotel on the Upper East Side of New York. The bride's dress is spectacularly expensive, but it is not made of yards of material; instead it is a couture sheath from a European designer whose exclusive name would be murmured around the crowd of sophisticated onlookers. The dress cost a high five-figure sum, but no one would even mention price because they know that is simply what such things cost. The dress is sleek and restrained, without any added embellishments. This bride's makeup and hair do not look very different from what she might wear to a cocktail party. She had her makeup done professionally, of course, but the main investment was in a variety of expensive laser and filler treatments. The bride does not want anyone to notice any significant difference in her appearance, so that her transformation seems natural, rather than purposeful and overt.

This upper-class social group understands that people who are trying to emulate their superiors put too much embellishment on the bride with little nuance, trying to show off what they could afford to an easily impressed crowd. The Pierre bride, however, knows to exercise restraint in her fashion and dress, even avoiding obvious brand designers in favor of handmade and unique creations, while at the same time using only the finest of materials. The bride's dress would cost more than the groom's attire, to be sure, but the groom is wearing an Italian designer suit, specially bought and tailored for the occasion. He eschews the morning coat as inappropriate for his lifestyle. This Pierre Hotel wedding is something that our upper-middle-class American family would not have the social training, financial ability, or aesthetic discernment to emulate. But they try.

5.2 Coffins and Their Creators

Not everybody in ancient Egypt made the same kinds of craft choices or moved in the same kinds of social circles. Other people, like the craftsmen of Deir el Medina in group 3, favored intricately painted polychrome scenes, but as craftsmen they could not afford much blue paint, not to mention orpiment.[4] Indeed, the Deir el Medina craftsmen understood high elite taste and discernment in their funerary arts because they themselves were responsible for creating it, decorating the tombs of the kings and the queens in the royal Theban necropolis. One group 3 coffin set belonging to a woman named Iyneferty and now in the Metropolitan Museum of Art (Cooney 2007; Hayes 1959) is

---

[4] Material pigment analysis of Deir el Medina tombs and funerary objects is limited, however see forthcoming work by Anne-Claire Salmas and Alexandra Winkels (personal communication, 2020).

illustrative of such social differences of discernment and ability (Figure 7a, b, and c). Iyneferty's title was "mistress of the house," or homemaker. Her coffin set included three pieces – a coffin, a one-piece mummy board, and a mummy mask made of cartonnage – fewer than either Ta-kayt or Henutmehyt. None of these coffin pieces show any gilding or glass inlay, a characteristic that Iyneferty's set shares with the rest of the coffins in her social group from Deir el Medina. None of the texts about coffin production from western Thebes mention gilding either. So, if their finances were so strapped, how could this coffin set have more in common with the high elites than the medium-level group?

The draftsmen used polychromy – red, white, black, blue, and green colored designs – throughout the entire set, showing the value of craft time over material. This social group understood that blue and green were valuable, but they made use of these colors within scenes and text spread judiciously throughout the coffin – not just on the upper body where audience members would have been focused during the Opening of the Mouth ceremony. Ostentatious display was eschewed. Like group 1, group 3 did not ignore parts of the coffin less visible at the funerary ceremonies. The bottom of the feet and the top of the head of Iyneferty's coffins received almost equal craft attention from the carpenter and draftsman as the head and chest, as if it would have been considered tacky within this community of practice to focus only on the most visible parts of the coffin and ignore the rest.

The mummy board of Iyneferty shows the deceased wearing a pleated white dress. Even though the coffin lid was painted in cheaper red and white paints, the draftsman was careful to show the close fit of the diaphanous pleated gown

(a) (b) (c)

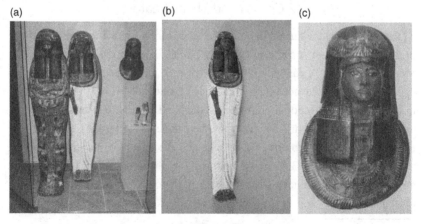

Figure 7a, b, and c – Coffin set of Iyneferty, 19th Dynasty, Metropolitan Museum of Art, 86.1.5a–c, 86.1.6a.

by skillfully painting layered stripes of red and white color, showing the appearance of the woman's body beneath draped fabric. Fine craftsmanship seems to have been the most important feature for this social group to display. This social group is characterized by artisanal work. To impress their colleagues, neighbors, friends, and clients, they needed to display their skills first and foremost. Blue and green paint never overshadowed draftsmanship. Fine materials never meant cutting back on other craft features. These men displayed what they had in abundance: skill, knowledge, and time.

The Deir el Medina artisans of group 3 decorated the tombs of royalty. As such, they were exposed to the funerary arts of the king and his family – not just what they created themselves in the Valley of the Kings or Queens – but all of the coffins and golden objects made at palace workshops when they were placed into the royal tombs. Every time there was a funeral in the Valley of the Kings or Queens, funerary objects were before the eyes of these artisans, conditioning them in the ways of elite social expectations of materiality. These craftsmen were not just seeing the highest tastes in funerary arts; they actually helped to form those tastes. And their exposure to high-level crafts from other workshops also formed their aesthetics.

These artisans earned additional money making coffins for the high Theban elite (Cooney 2007). They had to keep abreast of the latest trends in coffin styles for their wealthy patrons. Thus, the coffin set of Iyneferty, which was probably crafted by Iyneferty's husband and sons, may have been made partly as a calling card of craft abilities. All of the pieces had to shine and there was even-handed craftsmanship throughout the coffin set. The smaller of Iyneferty's pieces do not betray more detailed work than the larger. In fact, most of the detailed painting was lavished on the coffin, instead of the mummy board and mummy mask – by reason of its larger size as much as anything else.

The coffin group 3 of Iyneferty reveals lower elite people who could not afford the finer things in life, like imported woods, gilding, or even glass inlay – but who did have some disposable income to spend on their tombs and who understood what made a funerary object valuable to the very wealthiest people in all of Egypt. They needed a better understanding of what the high elite wanted in a coffin – even though there was no way they would have been able to afford gold or cedar or even orpiment.

To push this group 3 into the modern American wedding analogy is difficult, but perhaps the American academic intellectual fits the bill. They own education but not wealth, understand elite tastes but cannot afford them, keep their display carefully studied, overlooking no details, but cannot spend a nonexistent fortune. In our hypothetical wedding, an intimate group of forty-five gather in a small garden behind an Ethiopian restaurant given four stars by

Jonathan Gold in the *Los Angeles Times*. Overt displays are eschewed; the bride looks today as she would at a party. Her engagement ring is not a diamond, but a vintage 1920s' sapphire. Taste abounds even without a massive outlay of cash.

5.3 Coffins on a Budget

What about that fourth group? It is made up of ancient Egyptian people who could barely afford a decorated coffin. One Ramesside example comes from the British Museum and it belonged to a woman named Mutem-menu whose title also happens to be "Chantress of Amen," indicating that she held priestly duties of some kind in her local temple (Cooney 2007: 456–7), (Figure 8). Without additional text or other markers, we know very little about this Mutem-menu

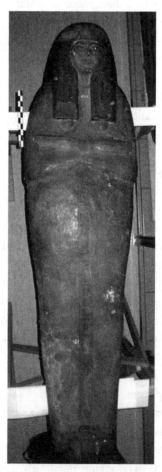

Figure 8 Coffin of Mutem-menu, Ramesside period, EA 6703, British Museum, photo by the author.

who was from a lower elite social group, like the wife of a simple wab priest or a land parcel owner.

Judging from lower status burials, this woman was lucky to have a coffin. Egyptian peasants were the mass of society and they were buried in group tombs, some with body containers, most wrapped in roughly woven shrouds or rolled up in palm rib mats. Even though the Egyptian peasantry made up approximately 95 percent of the ancient population, we know little about their tastes, their values, and their funerary beliefs and rituals, as most could not write their beliefs for us to read. Not until recently have archaeologists seen anything of value in recording burials of the poor. The remnants of the Egyptian peasantry's deaths have been ignored, poorly published, and left to looters and developers. This is the most elusive social group because we have no literary sources with which to reverse-engineer rituals and belief systems (Bruyère 1937; Grajetzki 2003, 2010; Niwiński 1996; Onderka & Toivari-Viitala 2014; Raven et al. 1998).

As far as we know, Mutem-menu did not own the pieces to make up anything resembling a coffin set, but since the coffin was not found in an excavated context, we cannot really know for certain. Maybe she did have a nesting set. What we can say is that the coffin has hardly any painted decoration. It was well carved, but it shows none of the careful undulations of the human body. The wood used by the carpenter was of poor quality and he used a great deal of plaster to fit the many pieces to one another. Most telling is the lack of decoration on this coffin. Only the eyes, mouth, and headband are painted. The rest of the coffin was left bare of imagery, probably because there were no funds left after the costs of coffin construction and carving. There is a text inscription, done in a different hand than that responsible for the painting of the eyes and mouth. This suggests that the family could not afford to pay a literate draftsman to paint the entire coffin. It is possible that the family of the deceased could not read the one hieroglyphic text on the surface. They would have known that text of any kind would be powerful and impressive to those in their socioeconomic group – because so many of them could not read either. This particular coffin might even have been reused, the older decoration simply smoothed away and left starkly undecorated.

The best wedding analogy to help explain this fourth coffin group is the afternoon church wedding at which only cake and punch were served in the church basement. The bride wears a cheap, discounted dress full of sparkle and sequins from Al's Formal Wear and the groom his own Sunday best suit. The bride's friends did her hair and makeup. Her engagement ring comes from the local mall.

By the same token, the social group of Mutem-menu could not afford fine materials or skilled craftsmanship. These people would consider themselves lucky to save the funds for the wood, plaster, paint, and craft time for the coffin. The craftsmen responsible for coffins like this were not as skilled. They may even have been itinerant, moving from village to village, making coffins for those who could afford them, because demand was so low. But we have no records for such low-level craftsmen because, unlike the top-level artisans of Deir el Medina who needed to record quotas for their most important client, they would have left no record of their craft activities except for the craft itself. The people who bought these coffins likely left no written receipt. In these modern days of easy factory-made materiality, it is hard for us to understand that not everyone could participate in ancient Egypt's complex system of material funerary practice. But make no mistake: the mass of Egyptian peasantry must have had belief systems that were less materially manifested, less textually reified, but more bodily understood and orally enacted.

6 The Coffin Craft System

Egyptologists have an extraordinary amount of social information about coffin production from the Ramesside Period, namely the preservation of the desert village of Deir el Medina, housing the artisans who cut and decorated the royal tombs in the Valley of the Kings and the Valley of the Queens (Bierbrier 1982; Černý 1973; Davies 1999, 2018; Janssen 1997; Valbelle 1985), giving names to ancient craftsmen who are so often nameless (cf. Jurman 2018).

Members of the royal work crew participated in private sector work, like high-cost coffin commissions, supplementing their income. Calculations suggest members of the work crew were able to earn much more than their state salaries making coffins and painting books of the dead for Theban elites, but they likely could not have brought in such commissions without a position in this royal workshop (Cooney 2007). Crew leaders, like scribes of the tomb and foremen, were in the most opportunistic social position, because they were in daily contact with the highest levels of the Theban elite, able to land those lucrative commissions. Whom you knew was everything; the higher the elite, the better the potential earnings.

We know more about the funerary arts trade at Deir el Medina than anywhere else in ancient Egypt, perhaps even more than anywhere in the entire ancient world. Thousands of texts preserve the details (McDowell 1999). Receipts recount the sale of funerary objects of various types and how the seller was paid. Workshop records kept by the craftsmen themselves document which object types they were working on, for whom, and how much each would cost. Letters recounted the travels of workmen to other locations for craftwork, requests for supplies, and updates on work. Sometimes funerary arts commissions were recorded in official texts kept by the scribe of the tomb, particularly if a workman took time off work to complete a project or if he was working on a commission with other crewmen. Legal texts tell us that funerary arts could be handed down to the next generation as part of an inheritance and that arguments over craftwork or price often had to be settled in court or before the oracle.

West Theban texts make the funerary arts market come alive, turning the Deir el Medina villagers into real people who were making economic decisions, who formed working groups, either with the official workshop or in informal groups of their peers, who trained their sons, who hired and fired their associates, and who held a unique social position in ancient Egypt. These craftsmen of Deir el Medina were not peasants; nor were they elites. They were skilled craftsmen, men with special talents and part of an unusual community of practice that made objects of death so that they could live. The Egyptian materiality of death created liminal social spaces.

6.1 The Craftsmen of Deir el Medina

This workshop of craftsmen was employed by the king, administered by the vizier and his scribal office, kept in a desert location close to their work, walled off and protected by *medjay* policemen, their comings and goings monitored (Burkard 2003). One could make the analogy to people working in the American military industrial complex today. Some such individuals work directly for the United States government at the Pentagon, but others work for a private company like Lockheed Martin, Raytheon, or the like, and they bid on government contracts competitively. Whoever they are working for, employees have to get security clearance and, in so doing, their lives are constantly examined for potential compromise. Their loyalty is put to question. There are complex protocols to "read" people into certain projects, so that individuals only know what they need to know, creating silos of knowledge with very few people at the top who have a handle on all the work that is being done in a given agency, even though those top people usually have little specialization in the nuts-and-bolts work that is being done.

Military spending is the largest single line item in the United States government's budget. Egypt likely spent a lot on its military too (Spalinger 2005), but Egypt arguably spent more on public works projects that proved in stone, plaster, and paint the infallibility and super-human nature of the king. When Deir el Medina was up and running, kings were no longer building pyramids but spreading their resources into multiple diverse projects, including additions to state temples all over the land, constructing their own Temple(s) of Millions of Years, their royal tomb in the Valley of the Kings, and their golden funerary assemblages. Given the amount of deposited riches that we know went into such tombs, such as Tutankhamun's burial goods, the inner workings of the royal tomb project were revealed only to a few elites.

The royal tomb was its own kind of manufactured intelligence, but of an ideological sort. To create it, artisans had to be empowered to construct the proof of the king's divinity while, at the same time, being separated from the rest of society lest the secrets come out, knowing they could not talk to anyone about the iconography and texts they were inscribing onto the tomb walls or mention the treasures installed into the tomb. The Deir el Medina artisans had their own kind of security clearance monitored and controlled by the vizierate and *medjay* policemen, in the same way a Raytheon engineer must submit to scrutiny to update their clearance or must pass soldiers' inspection when they move through security each day at the office.

Because of this level of secrecy and control, Deir el Medina craftsmen were well compensated. Their homes were provided for them, as was their food, water, and some necessities like oil and sandals (Davies 2018). They had health care (Austin 2014), domestic servants, perks and entertainment, funding for festivals, kind of like an American corporation buying out Disneyland for the company picnic day. This is likely why these artisans had the power to strike when they did not receive their pay in the 20th Dynasty (Eyre 1979; Frandsen 1990; Janssen 1992; Müller 2004). They knew too much. They were, in a sense, "the deep state" that the king needed to keep happy.

They also took on private commissions to build and decorate funerary arts, including tomb chapels, burial chambers, and coffins. Thousands of ostraca and papyri from the village and work sites clarify that while official work was the primary purpose of the craftsmen in this village, they had a secondary enterprise, using their skills, extra time, social network, and status in the community to gain commissions amongst elites in the private sector. West Theban texts tell us that artisans illuminated Books of the Dead, built and inscribed tombs and coffins, constructed canopic jars, and crafted decorated door jambs for private tombs for non-royal men and women who lived in the Theban area (Cooney 2007).

Where Egyptologists used to see illicit hustling, we now recognize a complex craft system with intertwined public and private sector elements, in which everyone on the work crew was actively involved in earning additional income. Where some Egyptologists saw the "exploitation" of artisans by the foremen and scribes who were supervising them, we can now see a cooperative venture in which the entire workshop participated.

People never record the whole story of their daily lives. Instead, they give us bits and snippets – a letter here, a last-will-and-testament there. And we must remind ourselves that the vast majority of ancient Egyptians left no records at all. Most ancient peoples remain silent. The craftsmen of Deir el Medina could write, but they did not sit about writing autobiographies or soul-searching diary accounts. For the most part, they only wrote something down when practicality drove them to it. These men produced laconic texts with no backstory – dates, names, activities, objects, lists of commodities, amounts of money, hirings, firings, debts, payments, deliveries, attendance, non-attendance, sickness, death, births, festivals, hymns, rituals, prayers, divorces, lawsuits, famine, demands for goods, and even threats, interrogations, and legal depositions.

6.2 How Did a Coffin Workshop Work?

Ancient Egyptian daily life texts record *things* and *activities*, not feelings or qualities; they record current states, not necessarily the reason that a given situation had come to that point. We do not have any texts that *explicitly* describe how the workshop at Deir el Medina worked – because they never needed to explain it to anyone, let alone themselves. To understand how these craftsmen behaved when they were not working directly for the king, we have to look at a wider variety of texts, including the thousands of receipts, craftsmen's records, legal texts, and letters from western Thebes that were not necessarily related to work in the royal work sites.

To understand why so much in the following pages is qualified by words such as "maybe" and "probably," it would be useful to imagine an archaeologist from the year 5000 CE trying to reconstruct the economic system of a small Texas town of 2000 CE – thousands of years after the United States has ceased to exist, thousands of years after people had stopped using American English – using only the archaeological site of a big-box store called Walmart, in an industrial area meant for petrochemical operations with a few offices and homes intact, accompanied by millions of scraps of paper that managed to survive because the town was in a very arid location. The archaeologist of the future would probably find thousands of fragments from the ledgers of what seemed to be a large employer, an oil refinery, including some of the payroll and a few workers' files, all leading to the conclusion that most of the economic activity in this town surrounded this one huge company. If the archaeologist of the future also looked at the thousand or so receipts from the Walmart, at the private bank statements, at depositions from malpractice lawsuits, and at the few contracts detailing business ventures, they would start to see that the economy of this town was very complex, that official and non-official business intersected with one another all the time, that even the skilled laborers in this refinery – the main community of practice – were active in building their own side businesses and financial ventures in which they hired co-workers and friends.

Any reconstruction of an ancient economy is based on fragments; if the researcher takes a holistic approach – looking at all the different types of texts – it is possible to build a series of circumstantial arguments about how that economy functioned. When Egyptologists first started to study the economy of Deir el Medina using its vast treasure trove of texts, it was easier to identify the records of official work in the king's tomb – the roll calls, the names of the guards on duty in the Valley, the delivery of supplies like paints, binders, and lamp wicks, the payment of wages by the office of the vizier, the amount of work that had been finished on a given day, the hiring and firing of craftsmen, the strikes by angry crewmen when wages were not paid, and the many letters to and from the vizier's office. These texts all pointed to a monolithic and centrally controlled institution – the royal workshop – and Egyptologists wrote almost all of their economic research about the official work in the royal tomb, seeing this as the entire economy when it was only a part (Bierbrier 1982; Demarée Mathieu, & Černý 2001; Valbelle 1985).

The state-controlled sector took precedence in the many articles and books written about Deir el Medina. Official work for a large employer has been easy to identify in the ancient texts. Because of the way our modern employment systems are usually structured – one job, one title, one paycheck – many of us might automatically assume that any private-sector craft activity had to be done out of sight of supervisors and was therefore of secondary importance. In the same way, we see the work in the king's tomb as the primary reason for the existence of the craftsmen's village of Deir el Medina. Private-sector craftwork is assumed to be a side business of little importance. But this perspective is skewed. Evidence-based study indicates that the workmen of Deir el Medina earned *more* in the private sector than they did working for the state. The many pertinent texts suggest that private-sector work was an integral part of the normal royal workshop and was the main means of ongoing support for these artisans. The state salary was about 11 *deben* a month (Mandeville 2014). The average price of decoration for one coffin at 10.5 *deben* could easily double that artisan's income for the month. Many other commissions – such as tomb painting work – would have paid more. Non-royal craftwork was an excellent way for most Deir el Medina craftsmen to make a living in addition to a state salary that was often late or underpaid, causing men to go on the occasional strike when the government got behind.

From this perspective, we see a village of craftsmen employed by the king to decorate his tomb but who were also allowed (or even encouraged) to earn additional income in the private sector. When doing their official work in the king's tomb, Deir el Medina craftsmen labored in a large group of some sixty men, organized into two groups according to strict military standards, in which each group was governed by a foreman and a scribe of the tomb (though sometimes there was only one scribe for both sides). Their work in the private sector was not so strictly organized. In fact, its flexibility, informality, and sometimes sheer disorganization are the reasons that Egyptologists have had such a hard time recognizing and understanding private-sector craftwork at all. The fact that private-sector craftwork coincides with and builds from state-supported craft communities further obfuscates the matter.

Skilled state artisans were commissioned by private clients to build coffins, furniture, or tombs. These artisans worked in small groups of one, two, or three men, not communally but sequentially. Their private-sector work often intersected with their official jobs: they used the official Deir el Medina crew to network potential clients, to find supplies, and to complete commissions. If we describe working in the king's tomb as formal and strictly organized, then crafting a coffin for a west Theban neighbor could be understood as loosely organized, messy, and hard to identify in the textual record. This non-royal craftwork should not be seen as pure entrepreneurism, because it was strongly associated with the resources of the official work crew, but it was close.

To see the economy of Deir el Medina, or of all of ancient Egypt for that matter, as a combination of official state work and private sector business is a useful perspective. For decades, Egyptologists have denied private enterprise or commercialism, arguing that the ancient Egyptians were too "primitive" to understand modern economic commercial activity, that without coined money they did not understand value, and they certainly did not know how to make a profit (Janssen 1988). Other Egyptologists have said that Egypt's economy was completely run by the state, even to the point of setting consistent prices for objects as mundane as clothing or sandals (Gutgesell 1982, 1989).

The seminal book *Commodity Prices from the Ramessid Period*, written by one of Egyptology's foremost Deir el Medina experts, Jac J. Janssen, is a tour de force of economic collection and hieratic reading ability. The book is filled with commodity types – clothing, leather goods, animals, furniture, coffins, food – and all the collected prices for each type of object, carefully culled from tens of thousands of west Theban ostraca and papyri. The Egyptians wrote down prices for all kinds of things, including loaves of bread, oxen, goats, asses, bundles of vegetables, tables, chairs, jewelry, linen shirts and shawls, huts, shrines, garden plots, and of course painted coffins, tombs, pyramidia, and funerary statuettes. To reconstruct these exchanges, Janssen pulled from scribbled receipts and workshop records on broken pieces of limestone and torn papyri, but even armed with this mass of evidence Janssen denied the existence of markets, profits, and private-sector craft activity, seeing only an economy that was primitive and/or state controlled.[5] It was Barry Kemp who pointed out that the ancient Egyptians could indeed barter in a market place with skill, thinking in terms of money even if they did not have coinage, making a profit with the sale of a crafted coffin or by leasing land at interest, explaining consistent prices for sandals or linen shirts in the market context of material and labor costs, working with supply and demand (Kemp 1991: 351–2).

Did funerary arts follow the same rules? Were they consistently priced? Looking at the collected prices for coffins, mummy boards, tombs, and illuminated Books of the Dead within their written contexts, we find complicated transactions involving five or six steps, in which disputes were recorded about particular prices, or for which complicated barter transactions set every commodity equal to an amount of grain or metal. The texts include useful details, because sometimes an object was rejected by its buyer as something not worthy of exchange, indicating that people *did* understand qualities that made commodities valuable (McDowell 1999: 76). The texts also preserved a wide range of value in the prices for crafted goods. Some coffins cost only 10 *deben*, while others cost more than 100 *deben*, meaning people could seek out objects of lower value or that they could decide to pay more for something because they thought it desirable and valuable. The demand for funerary arts created a market of income creation and adaptive exchanges, forming and shaping the larger Egyptian economy.

Those hundred or so West Theban texts pertaining to funerary arts production show an enormous amount of complex economic activity in this one small, remote, desert village of Deir el Medina. This reality must have been replicated in other places and times throughout Egypt – manifested by sophisticated and creative people, skilled in bargaining, intuitively understanding value systems and acting on their own initiative to set prices, working in both state and private sectors – but we lack evidence for those other systems.

It is not clear how much we can impose this west Theban economic system on other places and times of Egypt. Still, if one examined the west Theban texts without any *a priori* beliefs about the ancient Egyptian economy, that is, that it was primitive or state controlled or free and entrepreneurial, then most of us would be capable of recognizing a thriving market economy, in which people were constantly negotiating what they wanted with what they could afford to pay – just as we do every day of our lives. Complicated transactions were a testament to the ancient Egyptian villager bargaining hard for the price they

---

[5] For racism (subtle or overt) applied to ancient Egyptian datasets, see Reid 2002.

felt was fair. Price ranges provided the circumstantial evidence that not every coffin (or ox, or table) was the same, and that people understood nuances of value. Besides livestock, whose value waxed and waned, coffins were those commodities with the highest range of value. Price setting of grave goods resulted from complex negotiations between people with different agendas and with different social backgrounds and tastes. Tomb robbery, recommodification, and coffin reuse provide even more data to complicate a thriving funerary arts market.

The royal workshop probably allowed artisans to take on non-royal work orders – because it was through their official reputation that they could be located by elites, trusted to do the expensive and valuable task of creating funerary arts, and that their craftsmanship would be recognized as skilled and desirable. This secondary craftwork for the elite funerary market was not something that was discouraged by their superiors, but rather seems to have been de rigeur. In fact, it was probably the highest ranking men, like the scribe of the tomb and the foremen, who organized the most expensive orders with the highest ranking elites outside of the village – probably because they had the most intimate contact with the officials who reported to the king. The artisans of Deir el Medina built and decorated coffins, mummy boards, mummy masks, door jambs, statuettes, shabti figurines, amulets, stelae, and private tombs for anybody with whom they were in contact who could afford these objects. The textual information makes it clear that clients of funerary objects came from both inside and outside of the village.

Given this information from Deir el Medina, it is likely, although not proven, that many other royal workshops throughout Egypt – at the temple of Heliopolis, or at the palace of Memphis, or at Karnak Temple – used the same operational scheme: do your official work, do it well, and you would be able to use your title and reputation to make money in the private sector. Every major Egyptian temple probably had multiple workshops of some kind attached to it – some making "arts" like sculpted stone, or jewelry, or embellished furnishings, others making more utilitarian things like linen clothing, leather, chariots, or metal weapons. We can imagine the craftsmen in charge of outfitting the new king with leather armor for the battlefield taking private commissions from other elite families when they sent their son off to the front. Large state temples like Karnak would have employed dozens, probably hundreds, of artisans with a range of specializations – goldsmiths, bronze casters, carpenters, sculptors, and draftsmen – men who were able to carve and paint temple walls and who could craft cult objects made of wood and precious metals. Many of these artisans likely translated their state positions into additional earnings in the private sector, particularly in urban centers where elite populations, and thus potential clients, clustered.

Of course, one of the most frustrating things about studying ancient people is the uneven survival of evidence. Egyptologists are lucky to be able to read the archives of the Deir el Medina artisans, but, for the most part, the texts produced by other royal workshops do not survive. We know next to nothing about the daily work life of goldsmiths in Heliopolis, jewelry makers in Memphis, or hard stone sculptors in Aswan – during the New Kingdom or any other time. We do not know who produced the solid gold coffin and mummy mask of Tutankhamun. We do not know the living conditions of the relief carvers of sandstone and limestone temples built throughout the land. But we *do* know a great deal about the royal tomb makers of western Thebes – thanks to the remarkable preservation of their remote and arid village.

As members of the official crew, Deir el Medina craftsmen smoothed the limestone walls, cut the relief, and painted the scenes in the king's tomb. Almost all private sector funerary work at Deir el Medina, however, revolved around painting wooden objects – many of them funerary objects like anthropoid coffins and rectangular sarcophagi – for which they were paid a range of sums. Thus, although focused in their official duties on stone and paint, the same artisans could break free of these strictures and perform a wider variety of tasks that were in demand by clients in the private sector, including carpentry and painting on wood or papyrus. But the other reason these craftsmen focused on wood is because they had that material close at hand – not brought fresh from cultivation stands – but recycled from old tombs of the necropolis.

Why would a desert community so far from the river markets, not to mention stands of trees, housing experts in stone relief and painting, end up specializing in wooden funerary arts for the private sector? The village of Deir el Medina found itself at ground zero for private-sector coffin production when scarcity set in and access to fresh wood became problematic. Crisis created a new private sector niche for this craftsmen's village. The textual record from western Thebes circumstantially suggests that reuse was the source of wood. The 19th Dynasty preserves very few receipts for wood crafting and decoration. But during the 20th Dynasty and its concomitant crises, the situation changed and wood crafting exploded among Deir el Medina artisans – probably because this village was so close to the tombs and the new "raw" materials for such goods when the necropolis was mined for material by enterprising necropolis workers, guards, and tomb owners.

Indeed, one tomb at Deir el Medina, found intact by archaeologists and now called Theban Tomb 1, helps us to understand this point. The tomb was built by a 19th Dynasty man named Sennedjem, a "man of the crew" within the king's royal tomb workshop (Bierbrier 2001; Bruyère 1959a, 1959b; Haring 2006; Sanjaume 2006). Although it was poorly excavated and cleared with no drawings or photographs, we know that Sennedjem was buried in his burial chamber with about twenty other family members over the ensuing generations. Only nine of these individuals were found in their coffins by archaeologists, causing many, including myself (Cooney 2007: 240–50), to see social inequality within a family context – the poorer members of the family being buried with their wealthier cousins. Absence of evidence is not evidence of absence (Wengrow 2006: 154), and the tomb preserved so many mummified corpses without coffins that we might become suspicious about the possible existence of coffins, now gone. Only now that we have overwhelming evidence for coffin reuse in western Thebes can we potentially understand Theban Tomb 1 as a 20th-Dynasty end result after economic crisis had hit Thebes, causing the family that owned Theban Tomb 1 to recycle most of the coffins in their family burial chamber – either for their own family's funerary preparations, or to create new income for themselves in an exploding market for wooden tomb goods. The tomb owners did not reuse the coffin sets of their patriarchal ancestors and their wives, people like Sennedjem, his wife Iyneferty, their son Khonsu, and their daughters-in-law Tamaket and Isis, whose sets were (mostly) found intact by the tomb's discoverers. But other individuals in the family, lesser individuals, we must assume, were perhaps not so lucky. Coffin reuse, though it seems aberrant to us in terms of funerary morality, was just another negotiation within a vibrant private sector economy amongst creative agents who needed new sources of wood in the face of scarcity of materials. Coffin reuse was one of the most brilliant economic adaptations of the ancient world, and it took us over a hundred years of scholarship to recognize the village of Deir el Medina as ground-zero for this lucrative trade.

Sennedjem's coffin set, left in the tomb by his descendants, was made in the 19th Dynasty before the crisis set in, when fresh wood could still be acquired in Theban markets. His coffin set included a large and richly decorated wooden sarcophagus, an anthropoid coffin, a mummy board, and a cartonnage mummy mask. It is possible that he once owned an outer coffin that was removed and recommodified, but there is no way to know for certain, only the comparison with the burial equipment of his son Khonsu, which *does* include such an outer coffin (Figure 9a and b). Even if Sennedjem decorated all of these pieces himself, charging no one else for the labor, it is likely that a coffin set like his would have easily cost over 70 *deben*, a rough estimate based on the cost of wood for a normal coffin at 5 *deben* extrapolated to a sarcophagus and mummy board, plus some extra for pigments. How could a craftsman making 11 *deben* worth of grain a month have afforded to spend almost seven months' wages on

(a)

(b)

Figure 9a and b Coffin set of Khonsu, 19th Dynasty, Metropolitan Museum of Art, 86.1.1a–b, 86.1.2a–b, 86.1.4.

his funerary set while supporting his family? How could this craftsman afford the coffin and mummy board of his wife Iyneferty, not to mention his richly decorated burial chamber in addition? The most likely answer is that the craftsman Sennedjem did not earn only 11 *deben* a month. That was just his base salary from the state and the source of his reputation to acquire commissions decorating tombs and other funerary arts for wealthy Thebans. It was likely the same for his son Khonsu, whose (surviving) coffin set was larger than his father's, including not one but two coffins, a set that probably cost at least 100 *deben* in materials, with no labor included, though probably much more.

The expense of Sennedjem's and Khonsu's coffins indicates that funerary artisans were able to earn significant extra income *before* funerary reuse became prevalent. There is no evidence that these, or any other, 19th-Dynasty coffins were reused. There is also no evidence that coffins like these were somehow provided by the state for craftsmen like Sennedjem and Khonsu. We should assume they had to buy these objects themselves, and to do that they had to create the extra income. Perhaps they were selling their skills in tomb decoration in the 19th Dynasty in addition to selling funerary objects to the larger Theban elite community.

The economic information from western Thebes from the 19th to the 21st Dynasty provides a picture of change, not one of stability. Indeed, most of the west Theban texts find their origins in the 20th Dynasty, when things had become a decentralized mess of failed institutions and inconstant patrons, rather than a tightly controlled and centralized craft center. What had, in the 19th Dynasty, likely been a highly regulated group of specialized artisans, by the 20th Dynasty consisted of craftsmen taking on a variety of different craft jobs, far beyond their specialization in limestone cutting and painting to include woodworking and wood decoration for coffins. Make no mistake: Deir el Medina artisans also did woodwork in the 19th Dynasty, as texts do indicate, but not in the same amounts as in the 20th Dynasty.

Nineteenth-Dynasty Deir el Medina was characterized by generous state support and we have few private economic and legal texts. By the 20th Dynasty, more needed to be written down about private economic life or public work life because everyone was behaving not only opportunistically but also defensively, expecting disputes that demanded documentation and betraying patronage systems that had broken down. In the 20th Dynasty, there were arguably many more active economic agents than in the 19th Dynasty.

Arguing anything from absence is problematic, but in a village that preserved so much, it is telling that so few 19th-Dynasty texts exist compared with the mass of 20th-Dynasty documentation. When I first wrote about all of this economic activity in my book *The Cost of Death*, I did not know the extent of the funerary reuse that took place during the 20th Dynasty. This new evidence demands that we look at the village of Deir el Medina through a new lens, one of scarcity, but also one of funerary materiality demanding the creation of new markets for objects crafted from past interments.

The evidence indicates that by the 20th Dynasty people came to Deir el Medina (or sent word through an agent, like the Scribe of the Tomb) asking the artisans to paint wooden objects – like coffins, mummy boards, tables, doors, statues, and chests. There is even an abundance of prices for coffin *painting* in comparison to those for coffin *construction*, indicating a niche in painting wooden funerary arts, particularly coffins, but not in *building* those same objects. Wood had to be carried into Deir el Medina – either on a man's back or as part of a donkey's load. If you were trying to keep costs down, it may have been cheaper to hire a carpenter from another workshop – one nearer to the inundation lands where trees grew and where there were market places – and then bring the object to Deir el Medina for painting before its deposition in the necropolis. But if that were the case, why would elite people then transport these heavy objects – outer and inner coffins – all the way into the western desert to this isolated village near the secret Valley of the Kings to have them painted, only to ship them out again to their tombs in a different part of western Thebes? There must have been other painters in the Theban region, after all, artisans from other temple workshops who could do just as good a job painting objects.

The real reason there was so much work decorating wooden objects for the Deir el Medina artisans was precisely because these men had created a new market for funerary arts reuse when economic crisis hit Egypt in the 20th Dynasty. This community of practice had already been embedded in the burial ground for generations, occasionally commissioned to decorate private tombs and coffins. These same craftsmen could work with and for elite families and officials to open up unclaimed burial chambers in order to remove and process their contents, creating new income out of treasuries long since sealed. They knew all the secret locations where precious objects could be found. They knew all the guards (and thieves) who were engaged in illicit and sanctioned tomb openings, bringing coffins and other funerary arts into the light of day, to their village where, far away from prying eyes, the artisans could transform and update them into newly fashionable funerary arts. Given the numbers of reused coffins from the 20th and 21st Dynasties (Cooney Forthcoming-b), we must assume that most elite Theban families were engaged in this funerary recycling, opening their own and unclaimed burial chambers to recommodify old coffins (Cooney 2014b), much as the family descendants of Sennedjem had likely done with Theban Tomb 1 as an ostracon from the workers' huts proves that Sennedjem's burial chamber was opened and used for storage in the 20th Dynasty (Dorn 2011). Once their ancestors had been removed from their coffins to remain in the burial chamber, a family could reuse the wooden objects, bringing them to a nearby workshop – and what was closer than the necropolis workshop of Deir el Medina? – where objects could be stripped of their old decoration, replastered and repainted, either for newly dead family members or to sell on the market. Some texts, including the Tomb Robbery Papyri, do mention the "riverbank" as a marketplace where reused coffins could be sold (Peet 1930: 61).

Deir el Medina text evidence indicates that craftsmen pooled their skills when completing their non-royal commissions. In their private-sector work they labored together – sharing expertise in carpentry (or in locating and acquiring older coffins if that was the crafted wood source), plaster relief, wood cutting, and draftsmanship, sharing access to resources like tools, wood, paint, resins, wax, and plaster, and sharing various networks of communication, like connections to elite clients. This is not to say that this was some kind of idyllic artists' village coop in which all materials were part of a collective of equal players. Some artisans were better off than others; some had better connections and would have let everyone know their higher status. These men shared their *access* to materials, skills, and networks, but everything had a price, materially and socially. If an artisan needed wood and his neighbor required some Egyptian blue that the former happened to have on hand, then that was likely a good trade. If an artisan was not as skilled in carpentry, he could trade decoration for woodworking. If a craftsman had little access to elites of the larger Theban region, he could depend on the Scribe of the Tomb or one of the foremen to give him a commission he had put together – likely taking a cut for himself.

In fact, artisans produced thousands of ostraca about craftwork precisely because they were trying to keep track of who was using what materials and for whom within a decentralized and messy reality – to make sure that they got their due if they helped provide access, or recompense if they provided materials. Membership in the royal workshop decorating the king's tomb provided the craftsman with a reputation as a skilled artisan, but also with access to a vibrant network of fellow craftsmen to organize private-sector work for profit. And it was all occurring in the Theban necropolis – the absolute best place to acquire raw materials for funerary arts now that wood cultivation, glass making, and trade routes for other raw materials were compromised by the larger economic collapse at the end of the Bronze Age. Membership in this elite group ensured training, access to materials, contacts with potential clients among Theban elites, and apprenticeships for their sons, the future members of the royal workshop. If viewed in this way, the royal workshop was the chief means of support for the non-royal funerary arts market. The state workshop and private-sector crafts market were intertwined and interdependent. Their location close to the best materials for reuse was essential.

What do the ancient texts tell us about how coffin crafting actually worked? We might imagine one artisan building, painting, and varnishing one coffin at a time just as we imagine Leonardo da Vinci working on his paintings sequentially and in isolation. But this was not the way craftsmen did their work in Deir el Medina, not to mention Renaissance Italy (Baxandall 1972). There is actually no direct textual evidence that any one artisan made any one coffin from start to finish. Instead, it seems that one man constructed or acquired or modified the wood of a given coffin, then handed it off to another craftsman for plastering and painting, who may have then handed it off again to another for varnishing or other special embellishments. An ancient Egyptian coffin was produced in small groups of two or three men who did not work together at the same time but probably worked in their own homes or huts.

The creation of an Egyptian coffin usually began with a commission – an order from someone who wanted the object that ensured payment to the craftsmen for their time and materials. In other words, the artisans could not or did not want to make a coffin speculatively and be left with an object that no one wanted to buy. There are only the barest of hints of pure entrepreneurialism in which craftsmen had the extra cash to buy supplies and make a coffin to sell on spec in a marketplace. This may be hard for us to believe, given the certainty of death, but coffins were so expensive that demand was just too low to work speculatively.

In the 19th Dynasty, if craftsmen did make coffins without a buyer in mind, that is, entrepreneurially, they might have made only cheap, quickly produced coffins with low-quality wood and paint. They likely could not afford to risk any more investment than that. However, the tomb recommodification of the 20th and 21st Dynasties must have lit a spark, opening craftsmen of western Thebes up to entrepreneurialism like never before, leading them to source materials and build coffins speculatively, if only to hide the original source of an illicitly acquired coffin. Starting in the 20th Dynasty, wooden coffins must have appeared on the market with no previous order, with the hope that someone would purchase it who could not get reasonable access to wood by any other means. Elite Thebans interested in a large coffin purchase, who in the 19th Dynasty would perhaps have started a formal commission with a craft workshop specializing in painted wooden objects on the east bank, may have been driven in the 20th Dynasty by economic necessity to craftsmen embedded in the graveyards of the west bank precisely because they had access to the only available materials. Or, we can imagine if a family was reusing coffins from their own family sepulcher, the village of Deir el Medina was a most convenient place to drop off a coffin set for reworking.

Some texts suggest entrepreneurialism by ancient artisans. One text now in the Los Angeles County Museum of Art (O. LACMA M.80.203.191) (Goedicke & Wente 1962) mentions the Scribe of the Tomb Hori and "the commissions of the carpenters" that were meant for "the riverbank," suggesting that some woodworking was made on spec for the riverbank marketplace in the Theban region, ostensibly using resourced and recycled funerary objects from the necropolis. Another ostracon, O. LACMA M.80.203.193 (Goedicke & Wente 1962), reads:

> What the draftsman Neferhotep gave to Horemwia: 1 decorated stela of Nefertari, may she live. He gave to me 1 *meher* chest in exchange for it and also the decoration for him of 2 coffins for the riverbank. And he made 1 bed for me.

These two coffins are specifically said to be "for the riverbank," not for a particular person, suggesting they were not commissioned by a client but were meant to be sold to strangers on spec or to other artisans in need of wood and materials. Even if these coffins originated in reuse, there is the question: who would have purchased all those coffins that were so abundant by the 20th Dynasty at the riverbank market?

We can imagine even the rich driven to such markets to search out appropriate old coffins for recycling. Or perhaps they sent agents to do it for them given how undesirable it would be, as a well-known official, to go to a marketplace in order to pick over the available reused coffins for the correct fit, size, gender, and aesthetic qualities of the funerary equipment you wanted to order. The archaeological evidence is clear: everyone in Thebes, rich and poor, was deeply involved in coffin reuse whether they wanted to be or not. The social and ideological materiality of the coffin was too powerful for people to abandon funerary preparations just because there were no good sources of wood.

If a person was wealthy enough to order coffins in advance of death and they went to a craftsman to commission the objects, we know almost nothing about such a process. Did the client go to the craftsman or the other way around? The client was probably measured for fit in the coffin – although we regrettably have no evidence for such macabre and yet sensible practices. The prospective clients (because we can imagine that the entire family may have been a part of this process) probably sat down with the craftsman, or a pair of craftsmen, multiple times – with a few cups of beer – making sure they had established a bond. The texts do not preserve these human details.

Perhaps clients knew the craftsman through official connections. Or perhaps the reputation of the artisan was very well known and he was sought out. Our texts do not shed light on these aspects either. The first order of business would probably have included discussions of the number of pieces in a set, the amount of special embellishments like openwork cutting or raised plaster relief work, the amounts and locations of expensive paints, and the type of varnish, if any. If the coffin was made during the 20th or 21st Dynasties, we can imagine that the source of the wood might have been left unmentioned, the assumption being that these customers had come to the necropolis craftsmen for the obvious reason that it was the only place where you could get a coffin set made anymore. Or perhaps some elites mentioned the reused sources of wood freely, because they had opened up their own family's burial chambers to reuse the wooden containers of their ancestors. Such details about reuse were verbalized and not put into writing.

There are no texts that reveal human desires for particular coffin styles, aesthetic choices, or cost-cutting behaviors. There is one ostracon in Turin with the schematic drawing of a coffin on it. There is also an ostracon from the Metropolitan Museum of Art, New York (MMA 23.7.1) with a Ramesside coffin on its surface, found in the Valley of the Kings, and perhaps craftsmen used such sketches to discuss what the client wanted on their coffin and where. What we do have are laconic, matter-of-fact texts that give us the name of the client, the name of the craftsman, a date within a king's reign if we are very lucky, and basic instructions for the craftwork. For example, one ostracon now in Turin's Egyptian Museum and catalogued by Egyptologists as Ostracon Turin 57040 (Černý 1973) reads:

> Year 22, month 3 of spring, day 10. From the policeman Peniuemiteru: 2 pieces of large sycamore wood for Neferhotep, saying, "Make for me a coffin."

This section of the Theban text is actually informative and unmarred, an unusual feature for ancient ostraca – which usually provide no background information and on which 3000-year-old ink is faded and pieces of limestone have chipped away. This text clearly tells us that a policeman named Peniuemiteru visited a craftsman named Neferhotep and asked him to build a coffin for him. He also brought the wood with which to build the object. But, of course, we have no notion of what *kind* of coffin Peniuemiteru wanted, or where he got the wood, or how involved this process of commission was, and whether or not the coffin was for *himself* or if he was somehow involved in the craft process himself, as a middleman with mobility. This text leaves out something important: a price. We can only imagine that the haggling process would have been involved between client and craftsman, but it seems that this text documented the commission only, not the determination of price. Was the price agreed verbally? If so, why was it not written down?

A few texts suggest that some craftsmen had better access to clients and that they could "sell" these commissions if they had too much work to handle alone. In one case, a draftsman named Pay "gives" (which in the Egyptian mindset can easily mean "sells") some commissions to fellow artisans:

> Their commissions which are in the hand of the draftsman Pay: giving one to Paemheb [. . .] Giving one in order to bring Patjarbu [. . .] Total with are in the hand of the draftsman Pay: 4.

This ostracon (O. Deir el Medina 240) (Cooney 2007: 150) is broken in two places, and the context is far from clear, but it does suggest that the draftsman Pay had more private-sector work than he could handle and was selling four jobs to other craftsmen. The details of the work remain unmentioned, as does any payment changing hands. It is also not clear if this was Pay's way of documenting his sold commissions because he might still be responsible for delivering the finished work to clients. Maybe he was documenting this information so that he could get a cut of the price once the crafted objects were delivered, since he was the one who got the commissions in the first place. What we do know is that Pay had access to work that others did not and that he was recording the names of other craftsmen who took on the work. Circumstantially, this suggests Pay benefited financially and that the other craftsmen got work they otherwise would not have had. The fact that Pay was a draftsman by title is instructive, giving some indication that specialization on the crew allowed more power within the larger community and possibly more access to elite clients.

Other texts give us information about price. One ostracon, O. Berlin 12343 (Cooney 2007), tells us that the craftsman Bakienwerner was paid for both carpentry and drafting. The front side tells us about some of the painting he did:

> The decoration work from the workman Bakienwerner: the mummy cover of Mut-[. . .] making 12 *deben*, the outer coffin of An making 20 *deben*, and the inner coffin of An making 10 *deben*.

The text continues on the back with woodworking that this same craftsman did:

> The carpentry work which the workman Bakienwerner sold to the draftsman Horisheri: 1 plastered *debet* box making 8 *deben*, 1 *afdet* box making 2 *deben*, 1 coffin making 15 *deben* and the wood (for it) belongs to me, 1 small bed making 15 *deben* and the wood (for it) belongs to me, 1 bed making 20 *deben* and the wood (for it) belongs to me but the ebony is from his son Nebnefer.

We see that each object in this text was accompanied by a price – the amount which had already been paid or which was to be paid to Bakienwerner. If we look at these prices, we see a large range – presumably because some object types cost more than others and because some of the work was more time-consuming than others. For example, Bakienwerner constructed two beds – one for 15 *deben* and another for 20 *deben*. The different prices are briefly explained as the cheaper bed is said to be "small," while the other (ostensibly not small) bed included expensive ebony wood, presumably inlaid, perhaps even sourced from an 18th- or 19th-Dynasty funerary object found in the necropolis.

We also learn that even though the same artisan could perform both drafting and woodworking, he did not work on single coffins from start to finish, but as part of a craft collective. Individual artisans were able to make gains in the private-sector funerary arts market, but they still functioned communally. The composer of the text – perhaps Bakienwerner himself since he is mentioned on both sides – is careful to tell us when the wood was his, probably because he expected remuneration for it. And how did he acquire this wood from his desert location out in the necropolis so far from tree cultivation or Nile transport? Although we would never be told directly in such a text, this 20th-Dynasty individual may have acquired it from broken-down funerary objects resourced from old burial chambers.

6.3 The Cost of a Coffin

Craftsmen worked on objects in a range of values – from ridiculously cheap to very expensive. Writing the price next to the object was probably a quick and necessary signal to the craftsman in his own records – because it told him how much time and skill he should devote to a given piece. Never in these texts do we see labor accounted for in hours or other increments of time. But we do see many prices in copper *deben* in craftsmen's records, and it is likely that the ancient Egyptian artisan knew approximately how much work 15 *deben* meant.

We can also imagine that craftsmen knew how to remunerate risk and, although they never wrote it down explicitly, acquisitions of illicit wood probably came with a modified price. Or maybe some craftsmen just would not deal with certain materials (and dealers) at all because they knew they were simply too "hot" and that the larger social costs were too high.

Not every artisan in Deir el Medina, we can assume, was as skilled or as flexible as Bakienwerner who was able to perform both woodworking and painting. Many texts show carpenters trading wooden items with draftsmen who provided decoration. One ostracon in particular, O. Berlin 11260 (Cooney 2007), reads:

> The decoration which Horimenu did for Kaha: 1 coffin, its mummy board, and inside of it the wooden head. From Kaha: 1 *kniu* seat and 1 footstool making 13 *deben*, 1 *afdet* box making 1 *deben*, 1 *sheker* furniture piece making 2 *deben*, 1 wooden container making 3 *deben*.

We can see here that one artisan, specialized in painting, did decoration work on a coffin set in exchange for some items of furniture, likely undecorated and probably coming from a repurposed tomb somewhere in the necropolis, or perhaps produced by an artisan with access to fresh and untainted wood specializing in carpentry. Exchanges like this were common in the Deir el Medina textual material.

Craftsmen did not just exchange craftwork for other craftwork. These men did not think so one-dimensionally. In Deir el Medina with funerary materiality ready for reacquisition and repurposing, objects like coffins and boxes were treated like commodities, with values of their own, so that they could be bought and sold for livestock, clothing, or even immovable property like huts in the desert hills. One ostracon, O. Berlin P 12630 (Cooney 2007), records that a coffin was exchanged for an ox. This text is actually a deposition from a dispute:

> The scribe Amennakht, your husband, purchased one coffin from me saying, "I will give the ox in exchange for it." Now, he has not given it even today, and I mentioned it to Pa-aa-khet, and he said "Give one bed to me in addition (to the ox), and I will bring the ox to you when he is bigger." I gave the bed to him. The coffin isn't here, and neither is the bed even today. If you are giving the ox, then have someone bring it (to me). If there is no ox, then have someone bring back the bed and the coffin (which I gave to you).

This text sheds light on the ancient economic mind. This particular exchange seems to have gone wrong and was disputed by the women of each household (the person giving the deposition is speaking to the scribe's wife, not to him). It seems Amennakht had promised an ox in exchange for a coffin, but he never delivered the ox. When the seller complained, Amennakht tried to buy time, saying that he would hand over the ox once it had matured a bit more, thus taking over the expensive care and feeding of the large animal. In exchange Amennakht wanted another object – a bed – which was promptly and trustingly handed over by the unfortunate person who agreed to this deal. Amennakht still did not deliver the ox, and he now had a coffin and a bed in his possession for which he had never paid. The seller is justifiably miffed, taking the case to village authorities. We do not know the outcome of the dispute, but we do understand that coffins were thought to hold value, in this case as much value as an ox – the most expensive animal owned by families in the ancient Egyptian village (Janssen 1975; Cooney 2007).

If coffins held value as commodities, the materials used to make them – wood, pigments, and varnish – must have been expensive too. To earn additional money in the funerary arts market, craftsmen must have been on a constant lookout for easily accessible and good-quality supplies. One text, O. Brooklyn 37.1880 E (Cooney 2007), tells us that craftsmen could purchase wood at the riverbank market:

> (As for) the *menek* wood: I went down to the riverbank, and I had it brought out. I had the carpenter Sawadjyt see it, and he said, "It is worth 1 sack of barley." I sold it to his father, and he spent 1 month of days using it.

Whether the wood was freshly cut or came from repurposed and reused object(s), we cannot expect the text to tell us (because why would anyone highlight such problematic activities?). But this text does tell us that craftsmen could use the market on the riverbank – probably on the west bank of Thebes – to acquire raw or repurposed materials for craft production.

Wood was a particular problem for Deir el Medina craftsmen because they did not craft it in their daily work up at the king's tomb and because their village was located about a mile away from the inundation lands. If access to wood came from the necropolis itself, then their 20th-Dynasty preoccupation with wooden object decoration makes enormous sense. The best place, ironically, for access to wood was deep in the desert within community graveyards. The village of Deir el Medina was perfectly located – geographically and informatively – for acquiring that most scarce of resources. The ancient texts often specify the wood species, indicating that Deir el Medina artisans used native woods almost exclusively – wood like sycomore, acacia, tamarisk, and Christ's thorn. But a few ostraca mention ebony wood and other imported (and expensive) varieties. Cedar is only mentioned in relation to royal funerary commissions, never private commissions or sales (for instance O. Cairo 25504).

The Deir el Medina artisans likely kept a good supply of pigments on hand, given their daily activity painting the king's tomb. Not everyone in the village would have had the same access to state-provided pigments, and many texts indicate that the Deir el Medina craftsmen had to buy pigments, in some cases from each other. Some texts show the purchasing of these supplies in exchange for craftwork. One ostracon in particular, O. LACMA M.80.203.193 (Cooney 2007), records that the draftsman Neferhotep sold 6 *deben* of Egyptian blue pigment, 1 *deben* of yellow orpiment, and 1 silver *deben* of realgar red to Pashed – all in exchange for decorative work on a bed. These three were the most expensive pigments in the Deir el Medina palette. Egyptian blue was a bright frit. As for the arsenic-based golden orpiment and orangey-red realgar, a little went a long way.

Another text, O. Strasbourg H. 41 (Cooney 2007), shows a draftsman buying pigments and binders, like gum arabic used to make paints, presumably for private-sector craft production:

> What was sold to the draftsman Prehotep: 10 *deben* of gum, 20 *deben* of Egyptian blue pigment, 30 *deben* of *wadj* green frit pigment, 4 *deben* of *peresh* red lead pigment, 20 *deben* of *sheshiu* green frit pigment, 4 *deben* of yellow orpiment, 1 *deben* of realgar red pigment, and 5 *hin* of ochre pigments.

These pigments were mixed with binders or glues into the Egyptian palette of black, white, red, yellow, blue, and green, used to apply polychrome decoration and texts. One ancient text, O. Ashmolean Museum HO 151 (Cooney 2007), records painting work:

> The decoration which I did for him: 2 painted mummy covers making 6 sacks of grain, 2 decorated coffins making 20 *deben*, 1 mummy mask making 3 *deben* [. . .] the mummy cover of Henut-dju [. . .].

This text records the types of funerary objects, the number of funerary objects, the prices, and the names of people who owned or would own the objects, with little or no insight into the possible demands made by clients, the different socioeconomic backgrounds of the clients, the different styles desired by clients, or the choices made by the craftsmen. The Egyptians did not feel the need to write down such details, but it is easy for us to imagine that craftsmen and clients discussed these choices at length – what scenes they would include on the mummy's lower body, how much blue or green paint the client could afford to use, or where to put the most painstaking detail. One only need glance at the coffins themselves – in all their variety and nuance – to see that these discussions took place at all and that different individuals were making different stylistic and aesthetic choices.

After painting the coffin, varnish was applied, either by a varnish specialist, by the draftsman who had done the painting, or even by a carpenter. Opaque black pitch varnish was applied to the interior and underside of the coffin in the Ramesside period, while translucent yellow varnish was applied to the lid and sides. One letter (P. Deir el Medina 9) (Cooney 2007) tells us that a craftsman could demand varnishing supplies be delivered to him outside the village. Written by the "carpenter of the Lord of the Two Lands Maanakhtuef" and addressed "to the scribe of the vizier Amenmesu," it reads:

> I wish to hear how you are a thousand times a day because you did not visit during the year. Look, I am painting the inner coffin and the mummy mask, and the incense which you had brought has run out. Please have someone bring incense, pitch, and wax so that I can do the varnishing.

Another text, O. Deir el Medina 233 (Cooney 2007), tells us what a craftsman was paid, down to the last loaf of bread, for his varnish work on a sarcophagus:

> List of the property which the officer (of the crew) Djehutyhermetef paid to the draftsman Pay towards the recompense for the sarcophagus which was painted with dark varnish: 2 small *kebes* baskets, 2 small white loaves of bread, [. . .] of a gateway, 5 loaves of sunbaked bread, and thread for a *isha* garment.

Dark pitch varnish was a rich, glossy black; it evoked the *duat*, the realm of Osiris, and the fertile black soil of the Nile. Lighter yellow varnishes applied to the lid and sides gave the coffin its yellow glossy finish while allowing all the polychrome decoration to show through, giving the deceased the flesh of the sun god Re without having to use any gilding whatsoever.

From construction, to painting, to varnishing, Deir el Medina craftsmen were capable of creating top-quality coffins, but they lived in a remote village out in the desert, far away from the elites who could afford these objects. Deir el

Medina scribes and foremen were more integrated into the larger Theban regional community, particularly in their connections to officials in the office of vizier, the high priesthood of Amen at Karnak, and the administrators of west Theban funerary temples. For example, in P. Turin *Giornale* 17 B (Cooney 2007), the scribe of the tomb Horisheri put together a commission worth over 300 copper *deben*, one of the most lucrative funerary deals:

> Year 17 of the first month of winter, day 3. Making an account of the commissions of the West for the Chantress of Amen, king of the gods, Tanedjem in her house in Keday by the scribe of the tomb Horisheri and the scribe Khaem [. . .] and the scribe of the House of the Divine Adoratrice of Amen Mai-nehes.
>
> List of the carpentry and decoration done by the scribe of the tomb Horisheri for Tanedjem: 1 outer coffin making 60 *deben*, the decoration making 20 *deben* with the chiseling of its *shenu* for 5 *deben*, the hollowing of its *kebu* for 10 *deben*. Total 95. 1 inner coffin making 140 *deben*, its *kheneh* [. . .], its hollowed-out *kebuef* making 10 *deben*, the carving of its *shenu* with a chisel making 5 *deben*. Total 200. Total silver [i.e. money] being the carpentry and painting work: 295. 1 mummy board making 20 *deben*, its painting making 7 *deben*, the [carving] of its *shenu* with a chisel making 2, its hollowed-out *kebu* making 5 *deben*. Total 34 *deben*. All total silver for the coffins: 329 *deben*.

This text tells us about the "commissions of the West" or "funerary arts" that the high-ranking Scribe of the Tomb Horisheri brought back to Deir el Medina from three outside officials. Horisheri almost certainly had other craftsmen do the actual work. A scribe of the tomb is never documented doing carpentry or varnishing in our written evidence, and it is highly unlikely that Horisheri did all of this work himself either. But we can assume that he did negotiate with Tanedjem, or her representative, about the desired craft techniques for her coffin set (many of which are untranslatable) and their costs, bringing 329 copper *deben* worth of work into the village of Deir el Medina.

Despite all of this information – receipts, letters, legal texts, and memoranda – there is so much we still do not know about the funerary arts market. We do not know how far the Deir el Medina craftsmen could travel to get additional work. Some of the later 20th-Dynasty letters (in the Papyrus Deir el Medina collection) suggest long trips of twenty days' distance (Černý 1939). And some Egyptologists have suggested that Deir el Medina workers decorated the tombs of elites as far north as Saqqara during the 19th Dynasty (Zivie 2003). We know almost nothing about private-sector economic activities *before* the Ramesside period at Deir el Medina – during the 18th Dynasty when great rulers like Hatshepsut and Thutmose III ruled. We have almost no 18th-Dynasty textual material, either on ostraca or papyri, and it is not clear if the royal craftsmen were as active in the private sector at all. If we take the surviving tombs as an indication of their wealth, they were high earners. The 18th-Dynasty tomb of the royal architect Kha was found intact and his coffins were richly gilded – a luxury never seen on the 19th and 20th Dynasty coffins of the same village. In title and tomb, Kha had a vastly different status from later Deir el Medina artisans (Bruyère 1929, 1939; Ostrand 2013; Schiaparelli 1927; Vassilika 2010).

Even with these unknowns, Deir el Medina is the craft force we know the most about – thus revealing how much we do not know about the thousands of other craftsmen working in pharaonic Egypt. Did artisans in state workshops of the Old and Middle Kingdoms also make funerary arts for private, elite people? Even though such activities are likely (Chauvet 2008), we do not have any receipts or workshop records to give us any details. And what about the probable existence of unattached craftsmen in ancient Egypt – men who may have traveled locally from village to village, making low cost, cheap craft goods, including coffins, for people living in more provincial areas. The life of peddler craftsmen would certainly have been hard. Most orders would have consisted of cheap furniture like stools and beds. They would have been lucky to get a coffin commission for 5 to 10 *deben* worth of commodities. There would have been no time or need to take notes on ostraca, even assuming the unlikely possibility that craftsmen like this were literate. And without ancient texts, the only record we have of their craftwork would be poor-quality goods, like Ramesside coffins pieced together from over 100 pieces of wood, given minimal decoration, and inscribed with no texts (Raven 1991; Raven et al. 1998).

The commission and creation process of the Egyptian coffin was convoluted and multilayered, not a simple conversation between craftsman and buyer, but a complicated interaction between multiple craftsmen, possible middlemen, and buyers, not to mention the ancestors themselves, given all the objects recom-modified for reuse.

7 Coffins as Transactional Objects

Receipts are instructive documents. Some indicate that people had the ability to buy moderately expensive coffins of particular wood types. Receipt O. Berlin 14366 reads,

　　1　coffin of Christ's Thorn wood make [. . .] silver *deben*.
　　1　outer coffin making 40 [+x] *deben* [. . .]
　　1　carved (?) mummy board making 40 *deben*
　　Total silver *deben*: 5

The text gives us no names, but the coffin is said to be made of a special kind of wood – probably the same thorny wood that produced the jujube fruit, the Christ's thorn, or Ziziphus, also called sidder. The price comes to around 25 *deben* of copper, the average for the standard coffin in the west Theban documentation.

The receipt O. Michaelides 14 (Cooney 2007) indicates how craftsmen were paid for commissions with a variety of daily life necessities:

> Month 3 of inundation, day 29: What Nakhy gave to Neferhotep
> In exchange for the coffin of Iit-em-wau:
>   1 sack of barley and 3 *hin* of fat making 1 *seniu* (of silver), 1 sack of wheat
>   and 1 *sheker* basket making ½ (*seniu*), (1 pair of) sandals, an article of a *mendjem-nekher* sieve (?) making ½ (*seniu*)
> A *kebes* basket making ½ sacks (of grain).
> Total: 4 ½ sacks. Remainder: ½ sack.
> What Nakhy gave to Neferhotep in exchange for his coffin:
>   1 *tema* mat and 1 *sedjer* sleeping pallet making ½ (*seniu*), 1 *say* beam making ½ (seniu)
> That which he gave to me in exchange for the two shares which are in the pig:
> The *meku* food (?) bringing [. . .] making ¾ sacks, also [. . .]
>   2 *tema* mats, a *menedjem* basket [. . .] 2 ¾
> What the draftsman Neferhotep gave to Nakhy: a decorated coffin with paint, while he gave to me a pig making ½ (*seniu*) in exchange for it.
> Also a decorated coffin of Nodjmet. And it is his recompense that he gave:
> A *qeni* chair and the recompense of a decorated door frame.

Some of the commodities in this exchange remain mysterious (lexicography is vital work to determine the identity of particular commodities), but it tells us about the things that made the village of Deir el Medina tick – coffins and baskets, sleeping pallets and livestock, grain and metal. The exchange itself is confusing as four different coffins seem to change hands, allowing us to see how important such funerary arts were to the livelihood of these men. One was a coffin of a woman named Iit-em-wau bought by Nakhy for four and a half sacks of grain, equivalent to about nine *deben* of copper, a very low price for a coffin. Another coffin without any name cost one *seniu* of silver, equivalent to about five *deben* of copper, so even cheaper. For a third coffin mentioned, only the decoration is referenced, costing a half *seniu* of silver, around two and a half *deben* of copper, and the fourth coffin was said to be decorated for a woman named Nodjmet, for which a chair and a painted door frame were paid. No matter the complicated details, the coffins and coffin work are partial and cheap, on average, while the other commodities – the chairs and sleeping pallets and grain and fat – were the big-ticket items for the buyers involved. Receipts demonstrate how easily the ancient Thebans thought in terms of money even though they did not use coinage. They could, in one exchange, move between different equivalencies of value – sacks of grain, weights of metal, not to mention a variety of different commodities. This was a savvy village economy.

7.1 Reconstructing a Coffin Commission

But receipts can only tell us so much. A hypothetical reconstruction of one such receipt can help us see how much of the ancient human context we are missing. Imagine for a moment that you are the chief of police of the necropolis. Today one of the tomb craftsmen – Khnummose – is delivering the coffin you commissioned from him. It is the reign of Ramses Nebmaatre-Meryamun (you have no idea that he will one day be called Ramses VI). You call out to your wife as you approach the house. She comes running out, along with five of her friends, who all start oohing and aahing over the shiny new coffin. She seems pleased with it and tells you that she will make a fine Osiris when the day comes.

Khnummose and his sons have finished unloading the coffin from the donkey and the negotiation begins. Khnummose starts by asking you if you think the coffin is worth the 25 *deben* you agreed to when you commissioned the object. You assent readily, saying that it is a fine coffin, just as promised, with careful carving and painting. But you add that you have done many favors for the necropolis village and that you hope Khnummose can give you a break on the price. He knew this was coming and so he quickly agrees, saying "22 *deben*?" You raise an eyebrow and give him your best chief-of-police stare, and he says "Okay, 20 *deben*. That is more than fair." You agree and you are off to a good start.

You ask Khnummose what commodities he is most in need of. Khnummose says that he will really take just about anything, because the vizier's office has not delivered supplies in months. Having said that, he quickly adds that linens are in short supply. You catch your wife's eye and she hurries to fetch some of the linens she has woven. When the textiles are brought out to the courtyard, Khnummose examines the craftsmanship critically. "Smooth-quality?" he asks. You nod.

As Khnummose examines the linens, you call out to your fellow villagers to bring any extra commodities they might have on hand. Your cousin brings some of his leatherwork out to the courtyard for Khnummose to see. Your brother has a few goats that he could part with, and they join the group. And his wife has a number of palm-rib mats that she has just finished weaving.

Khnummose sees all of this activity but is still examining the linens. He sets aside some of the shirts, saying "I'll have three of these." You both know that new smooth-quality shirts are worth five *deben* apiece. That price does not change much – unless the shirt is worn and mended. Neither of you say it, but you know he's just agreed to take the shirts for 15 *deben* of the 20 *deben* price. Then he says, "How much for the sheets?" Your wife answers proudly, "No less than 10 *deben*," which you know is more than fair. But Khnummose has just shown that he is willing to move beyond the original deal and says, "What if I added some jars of fresh fat to the deal? We've just butchered an ox in the necropolis village, and I've got one and a half jars in my share."

"Yes, good," you say, and Khnummose prods his son to go run and fetch the fat. He knows, like everyone else, that the deal will run smoother for him if the jars of fat are there on the ground with all the other objects. Too many people promise to pay during a deal, but then never deliver.

Khnummose puts aside some sandal thongs from Penpamer's leatherwork into a pile and starts to consider a wooden bed. Khnummose and your cousin Penpamer then break out into a heated discussion over the cost of the bed. While the two of them are busy sorting out their side transaction, you see that one of your subordinates, the policeman Amenkhau, is bringing over some sesame oil that his family in the next village has just pressed. It is good quality and Khnummose seems interested. He puts aside some jars of it into his growing pile of goods. The policeman's wife then shows Khnummose one of her linen sheets, which she grandly tells him she can sell for only eight *deben*. You watch your own wife sneer at this, but Khnummose is more than interested in the bargain and adds the sheet to his pile, to your wife's dismay. Then one of the water carriers sees his opportunity and shoves some of the marsh plants he's just collected under Khnummose's nose. Those plants are pretty hard to come by in the necropolis village so far from the river, and you notice him toss two huge bunches into his pile.

Your wife is entering the fray again, this time with some sandals that her father made. They are decent quality, worth about two *deben* each. The vizier has not made any sandal deliveries in a while. You notice the worn sandals Khnummose is wearing. He grunts and throws two pairs onto his pile.

When the boy finally comes back with the jars of fresh fat, Khnummose opens the jars and examines the amount. "It's a bit more than one and a half jars. How about 48 *deben*?" he says. You peer into the fragrant jars and say, "well, just a bit. How about 46 *deben* for the whole?" This seems to appease Khnummose. He knows that one jar of fresh fat usually goes for 30 *deben*. One and a half jars would be 45 so he has just gotten an extra *deben* added to his deal.

So, both of you stand back and start to survey the scene. Khnummose is selling you a coffin for 20 *deben* plus one and a half jars of lard for 46. So, he is going to want 66 *deben* worth of goods. Three of your wife's shirts, some sandal thongs, two pairs of sandals, that wooden bed, a few jars of sesame oil, that linen sheet, and two massive bundles of marsh plants. Khnummose is more than thirty *deben* over.

This sparks a frenzy. Your cousin Penpamer suddenly shows up with heavy jar. He tells Khnummose that it is almost a full *hin* jar of fresh mutton fat, a cheaper kind that will go a long way in the necropolis village. They agree to nine *deben*. Khnummose is still 25 *deben* over, but there's nothing left in the village that he really wants. You tell Khnummose that you have two *deben* worth of real copper that you can give him in good faith to seal the deal until you can pay the remainder. And you suggest that he draw up a receipt. Khnummose assents, surveys the goods, and writes down the trade:

> List of all the objects that the crewman Khnummose sold to the chief of police: Nebsemen, son of Raia: 1 ½ *hin* jars of fresh fat, 1 coffin making 20 *deben*.
>
> From Nebsemen: 3 smooth-quality shirts making 15 *deben* and 2 copper *deben*.
>
> From Penpamer: 3 sandal thongs.
>
> From Penpamer: 2 *hin* jars of fresh fat. From him: 1 bed making 15 *deben*.
>
> From the policeman Amenkhau: 2 *hin* jars of sesame oil, 1 smooth-quality sheet making 8 *deben*.
>
> From the water carrier Amenkhau: 2 items of *sesed* plant making 4 *deben*.
>
> From Nebsemen: 2 pairs of sandals.
>
> Total copper: 66.

And after drying the ostracon by blowing on it and sprinkling it with sand, he flips it over and documents that he paid too much: "Amount of money from Khnummose with Nebsemen: 66 copper *deben*. Paid from him: 43 copper *deben*. The remainder: 23." He shows you the text and you nod. Most of the other villagers cannot read at all, but you can make your way through a text like this.

The scene above is one way to imagine the receipt now known as Ostracon Ashmolean 162 (Cooney 2007) (Figure 10). When receipts were written up, all they needed to write down were the bare necessities: names, object types, amounts, and circumstances of the trade. Everybody involved already knew the details. But some texts, like this one, suggest very complicated human negotiations.

Figure 10 Ostracon inscribed with economic information, limestone, Egypt, 19th Dynasty, year 2, probably of Merneptah. O. LACMA M.80.203.193, Los Angeles County Museum of Art (www.lacma.org).

8 How Coffins Formed Egyptian Society

The coffin formed an Egyptian society of craftsmen and necropolis workers. But to what extent? To approach that answer we need to investigate coffin demand. Can the available evidence tell us how many coffins were made in 19th- and 20th-Dynasty Thebes? The Ramesside period has preserved fewer than 100 total coffins, including fragments; the 21st Dynasty has preserved more, almost 1,000 total coffins, but these numbers don't help us reconstruct coffin demand, only reuse patterns and the vagaries of archaeological preservation. Let's look at the price data. In theory, an artisan could double or triple his state income by creating one coffin a month. But if we assume that each of the approximately 40 workmen at Deir el Medina – and sometimes there were 60 or 120 of them – could create one coffin a month, they would have crafted about 500 coffins each year for the Theban region, resulting in some 60,000 coffins hypothetically for the 19th and 20th Dynasties. The archaeological record simply does not allow for such a high number, even including the thousands of fragments of coffins waiting to be discovered or lying unpublished in magazine storage. Coffin demand supported a smaller and privileged class of craftsmen.

Coffins were made sequentially by more than one craftsman: one to do the woodworking and another to decorate it. If we return to our analogy of the American Industrial Complex with each defense contract performed by a collective of engineers, administrators, attorneys, accountants, and security, this is exactly what we see in the Deir el Medina artisans' system of funerary arts production for the private sector. If each workman was doing *some kind* of work on one coffin a month, Deir el Medina craftsmen could collectively produce about 250 coffins in one year, equal to coffin sets for about 150–200 people, still a very high number given the known local elites in the Ramesside period. The west Theban documentation preserves only 168 prices for coffins and 37 prices for additional funerary elements, such as canopic equipment, shabtis, Books of the Dead, and tomb decoration, during about 250 years of activity. Even if we assume that the majority of prices are not preserved in the remaining textual record of ostraca and papyri, it is highly unlikely that there was economic demand for the production of 250 coffins *every year*. Tomb data corroborates a limited number of Theban elites able to afford coffins.[6]

It seems more likely that craftsmen received a coffin commission every other or every third month, suggesting that Deir el Medina produced as many as 80–120 coffins and/or coffin elements a year, for about 40–100 individuals, assuming that the 40 or so members would have received a commission four to six times a year if it required at least two men to finish each coffin. Deir el Medina workmen also occasionally created and decorated private tombs for wealthy Thebans, that is, much larger commissions (Cooney 2008b). This entire industry of funerary production was created for a few dozen wealthy families, the core of social power in ancient Thebes.

Those few wealthy Thebans situated themselves amongst a material assemblage of wood, plaster, paint, natron, resins, and embalmed corpses within a competitive arena. They demanded artisanal communities of practice to craft, display, and deposit their social bodies, revealing "how ritual commerce between the living and the dead structured the wider organisation of labour and consumption over time" (Wengrow 2006: 76). Thus, it's not just that Egyptologists get most social information from graveyards (Wengrow 2006: 6), but also that these ancestor-places and ancestor-continuity allowed and then demanded ongoing interaction by means of ancestor-materiality. The deposition of ancestors into the grave provided a social theater for elites to materially consume, anchoring

---

[6] Although based on outdated Porter and Moss reign assignments, it has been estimated that about eight decorated private tombs were constructed in the Theban necropolis every decade during the New Kingdom for high-level elites – that is, a little less than one per year (Romer 1988). If we assume that an equal number of undecorated tombs were finished in the same ten-year time span for lower-level elites, and if we assume that each tomb equaled a family of four, which is rather conservative, then about sixty-four nobles required burial every ten years. This is a very low number, but it still does not account for the much lower number of decorated chapels and burial chambers created during the later New Kingdom, when necropolis security was threatened and when elites may have had more money to invest in coffins, because they did not have to spend huge amounts on private tomb decoration, nor on wood.

them to specific places and status positions. It is the materiality that helps us to identify how few people held social power in Ramesside Thebes, not to mention how trapped those elites were in their own constructed theater of display, doing anything to maintain their social place, even committing theft and reuse. The dichotomy between humanity and materiality only exists if you somehow see humans as unnatural (Steiner 1999).

Thebans had been interring their dead into west bank spaces for generations, creating "a density of social memory more vital than the massing of permanent dwellings." This was that "ritual commerce with the dead" (Wengrow 2006: 83) and, when coffin reuse became de rigeur, those same ancestors had to give their funerary materiality to the larger social cause. Funerary arts were such an important part of social identity that when pressed with scarcity, the Egyptians decided, en masse, according to reuse percentages of over 60 percent in the current sample, to recycle their ancestors' tombs and coffins (Cooney Forthcoming-b). Whether that act was perceived as willingly or unwillingly done, funerary objects that had once been deposited individually and permanently in decorated tombs for each patriarch were now interred communally and impermanently, reifying contemporary social circumstances by means of constant interaction with the dead. Some of Egypt's ancestors must have been purposefully maintained in their tomb spaces to claim vital social connections in this age of unrest – like Khonsu and Sennedjem who were maintained in Deir el Medina's Theban Tomb 1 – cementing and reifying power lineages through the materiality of tombs, coffins, and embalmed bodies. In the case of Sennedjem's family, the maintenance of these ancestors may have established a lock on a place in the Deir el Medina crew during crisis. Time is power; things are power; established material continuity is difficult to subvert. Whether their funerary materiality was reused or maintained, physical ancestors could be guarantors of social claims.

If coffins broadcast connections to your people and your politics, then crisis demanded adaptations through that materiality (Bloch & Parry 1982). In the Ramesside period, a new variability of coffin iconography coincided with economic upheaval and we need to put this new commissioner choice of scene and iconography into dialogue with intense social change. Complicated coffin iconography coincided with a simplification (Wengrow 2006: 151) of the overall burial assemblage in the 20th Dynasty – smaller, portable coffins, unmarked and undecorated tombs, and abandonment of hoarded commodities (Niwiński 1988). A newly complicated coffin iconography broadcast who held restricted religious knowledge and who did not, while also creating a busy palette under which to hide coffin reuse. Increased funerary simplification fit with the zeitgeist of the times because Theban (or Tanite) leaders could not flaunt extravagance while their people suffered lack. In the end, the rich were controlled by their precious things.

References

Allen, J. P. 1988. *Genesis in Egypt: The Philosophy of Ancient Egyptian Creation Accounts*. San Antonio, TX: Van Siclen Books for Yale Egyptological Seminar, Yale University.

Allen, J. P. 2006. *The Egyptian Coffin Texts, Volume 8: Middle Kingdom Copies of Pyramid Texts*. Vol. 132, Oriental Institute Publications. Chicago: University of Chicago Press.

Amenta, A. and Guichard, H. (eds.) 2017. *Proceedings First Vatican Coffin Conference 19–22 June 2013*. Vatican City: Edizioni Musei Vaticani.

Appadurai, A. 1986. *The Social Life of Things: Commodities in Cultural Perspective*. Cambridge: Cambridge University Press.

Arbuckle MacLeod, C. Forthcoming. "Transformations in the materiality of death: rishi coffins and the Second Intermediate Period." In Amenta, A. and Capozzo M. (eds.) *Proceedings of the Second Vatican Coffins Conference*. Rome: Musei Vaticani.

Arnold, J. and Lang, U. 2007. Changing American home life: trends in domestic leisure and storage among middle-class families. *Journal of Family and Economic Issues*, 28, 23–48.

Assmann, J. 2005. *Death and Salvation in Ancient Egypt*. Ithaca, NY: Cornell University Press.

Aston, D. A. 2009. *Burial Assemblages of Dynasty 21–25. Chronology – Typology – Developments*. Vienna: Verlag der Österreichischen Akademie der Wissenschaften.

Austin, A. 2014. Contending with illness in Ancient Egypt: a textual and osteological study of health care at Deir el-Medina. PhD thesis: University of California Los Angeles.

Barwik, M. 1999. Typology and dating of the "white"-type anthropoid coffins of the early XVIIIth Dynasty. *Études et Travaux*, 18, 7–33.

Baxandall, M. 1972. *Painting and Experience in Fifteenth-Century Italy: A Primer in the Social History of Pictorial Style*. Oxford: Oxford University Press.

Bayer-Niemeier, E., Borg, B., Burkard, G. et al. 1993. *Skulptur, Malerei, Papyri und Särge*. Melsungen: Gutenberg.

Bettum, A. 2011. Faces within faces: The symbolic function of nested yellow coffins in Ancient Egypt. PhD thesis: University of Oslo.

Bierbrier, M. L. 1982. *The Tomb Builders of the Pharaohs*, Cairo: American University in Cairo Press.

Bierbrier, M. L. 2001. The Tomb of Sennedjem. In Weeks, K. R. (ed.) *Valley of the Kings: The Tombs and the Funerary Temples of Thebes West*. Cairo: American University in Cairo Press.

Bloch, M. and Parry, J. 1982. *Death and the Regeneration of Life*. Cambridge: Cambridge University Press.

Boivin, N. 2008. *Material Cultures, Material Minds: The Impact of Things on Human Thought, Society, and Evolution*. Cambridge: Cambridge University Press.

Bourdieu, P. 1984. *Distinction: A Social Critique of the Judgement of Taste*. Translated by R. Nice. Cambridge, MA: Harvard University Press.

Broekman, G. P. F., Cooney, K. M., Amenta, A., et al. (eds.) 2018. *The Coffins of the Priests of Amun: Egyptian Coffins from the 21st Dynasty in the Collection of the National Museum of Antiquities in Leiden*. Leiden: Sidestone; Rijksmuseum van Oudheden.

Bruyère, B. 1929. *Rapport Sur Les Fouilles de Deir el Médineh (1928)*. Vol. 6. Fouilles de L'Institut français d'archéologie orientale. Cairo: L'Institut français d'archéologie orientale.

Bruyère, B. 1937. *Rapport Sur Les Fouilles de Deir el Médineh (1934–1935). Deuxième Partie: La Nécropole De L'Est*. Cairo: L'Institut français d'archéologie orientale.

Bruyère, B. 1939. *La Chapelle de Khâ*. Cairo: MIFAO 73.

Bruyère, B. 1959a. *La Tombe n° 1 de Sen-nedjem à Deir el Médineh*, Cairo: L'Institut français d'archéologie orientale.

Bruyère, B. 1959b. *La Tombe no. I de Sennedjem à Deir el Médineh*, Cairo: L'Institut français d'archéologie orientale.

Bryce, T. 2003. *Letters of the Great Kings of the Ancient Near East: The Royal Correspondence of the Late Bronze Age*. Abingdon, UK: Routledge.

Bryce, T. 2009. *The Routledge Handbook of the Peoples and Places of Ancient Western Asia: The Near East from the Early Bronze Age to the Fall of the Persian Empire*. Abingdon, UK: Routledge.

Burkard, G. 2003. "... Die im Dunkeln sieht man nicht": Waren die Arbeiter im Tal der Könige privilegierte Gefangene? In Bommas, M., Guksch, H. and Hofmann, E. (eds.) *Grab und Totenkult im Alten Ägypten*. München: Beck, 128–46.

Cavilier, G. 2017. The Butehamun Project: research on the funerary equipment. In Amenta, A. and Guichard, H. (eds.) *Proceedings of the First Vatican Conference 19–22 June 2013*. Vatican City: Edizioni Musei Vaticani, 97–100, 576–7.

Černý, J. 1939. *Late Ramesside Letters*. Brussels: Fondation Égyptologique Reine Élisabeth.

Černý, J. 1973. *Community of Workmen at Thebes in the Ramesside Period.* Cairo: L'Institut français d'archéologie orientale.

Chauvet, V. 2008. Decoration and architecture: the definition of private tomb environment. In D'Auria, S. H. (ed.) *Servant of Mut: Studies in Honor of Richard A. Fazzini.* Leiden: Brill, 44–52.

Ciampini, E. M. 2017. Notes on the inscribed Old and Middle Kingdom coffins in the Egyptian Turin Museum. In Guidotti, M. C. and Rosati, G. (eds.) *Proceedings of the XI International Congress of Egyptologists*, Florence Egyptian Museum, Florence, August 23–30, 2015. Oxford: Archeopress, 103–6.

Clark, A. and Chalmers, D. 1998. The extended mind. *Analysis*, 58, 7–19.

Clark, J. E. and Parry, W. J. 1990. Craft specialization and cultural complexity. *Research in Economic Anthropology*, 12, 289–346.

Cline, E. 2014. *1177 B.C.: The Year Civilization Collapsed.* Princeton: Princeton University Press.

Cline, E. H. 1994. *Sailing the Wine-Dark Sea: International Trade and the Late Bronze Age Aegean.* Oxford: Tempus Reparatum.

Cline, E. H. and O'Connor, D. B. 2012. The sea peoples. In Cline, E. H. and O'Connor, D. (eds.) *Ramesses III: The Life and Times of Egypt's Last Hero.* Ann Arbor: University of Michigan Press, 180–208.

Connor, S. 2018. Sculpture workshops: who, where and for whom? In Moreno García, J. C., Quirke, S., Miniaci, G. and Stauder, A. (eds.) *The Arts of Making in Ancient Egypt: Voices, Images, and Objects of Material Producers 2000–1550 BC.* Leiden: Sidestone, 11–30.

Cooney, K. M. 2007. *The Cost of Death: The Social and Economic Value of Ancient Egyptian Funerary Art in the Ramesside Period.* Leiden: Egyptologische Uitgaven.

Cooney, K. M. 2008a. The fragmentation of the female: re-gendered funerary equipment as a means of rebirth. In Graves-Brown, C. (ed.) *Sex and Gender in Ancient Egypt.* Swansea: Classical Press of Wales, 1–25.

Cooney, K. M. 2008b. Profit or exploitation? The production of private Ramesside tombs within the West Theban funerary economy. *Journal of Egyptian History*, 1, 79–115.

Cooney, K. M. 2011. Changing burial practices at the end of the New Kingdom: defensive adaptations in tomb commissions, coffin commissions, coffin decoration, and mummification. *Journal of the American Research Center in Egypt*, 47, 3–44.

Cooney, K. M. 2014a. Ancient Egyptian funerary arts as social documents: social place, reuse, and working towards a new typology of 21st Dynasty coffins. In Sousa, R. (ed.) *Body, Cosmos, and Eternity: New Research Trends in the Iconography and Symbolism of Ancient Egyptian Coffins.* Oxford: Archaeopress, 45–66.

Cooney, K. M. 2014b. Private sector tomb robbery and funerary arts reuse according to West Theban documentation. In Toivari-Viitala, J., Vartiainen, T. and Uvanto, S. (eds.) *Deir El Medina Studies: Helsinki June 24–26 2009, Proceedings.* Helsinki: The Finnish Egyptological Society, Occasional Publications 2, 16–28.

Cooney, K. M. Forthcoming-a. Making Egypt great again: Egypt under the Ramessides. In Moeller, N., Potts, D. T. and Radner, K. (eds.) *The Oxford History of the Ancient Near East.* Oxford: Oxford University Press.

Cooney, K. M. Forthcoming-b. *Recycling for Death: A Social History of Ancient Egypt Through Coffins of Dynasties 19–22.* Cairo: The American University in Cairo Press.

Costin, C. L. 1991. Craft specialization: issues in defining, documenting, and explaining the organization of production. In Schiffer, M. B. (ed.) *Archaeological Method and Theory.* Tucson: University of Arizona, 1–56.

Costin, C. L. and Wright, R. P. (eds.) 1998. *Craft and Social Identity,* Archaeological papers of the American Anthropological Association, Vol. 8. Arlington, VA: American Anthropological Association.

Cowan, R. S. 1983. *More Work for Mother: The Ironies of Household Technology from the Open Hearth to the Microwave.* New York: Basic Books.

Davies, B. G. 1999. *Who's Who at Deir el-Medina: A Prospographic Study of the Royal Workmen's Community.* Leiden: Egyptologische Uitgaven.

Davies, B. G. 2018. *Life Within the Five Walls: A Handbook to Deir el-Medina.* Wallasey, UK: Abercromby Press.

Demarée, R. J., Mathieu, B. and Černý, J. 2001. *A Community of Workmen at Thebes in the Ramesside Period.* Cairo: Institut français d'archéologie orientale.

DeMarrais, E., Gosden, C. and Renfrew, C. 2004. *Rethinking Materiality: The Engagement of Mind with the Material World.* Oakville, CT: McDonald Institute for Archaeological Research.

Dorn, A. 2011. *Arbeiterhütten im Tal der Könige: Ein Beitrag zur Altägyptischen Sozialgeschichte Aufgrund von Neuem Quellenmaterial aus der Mitte der 20. Dynastie (ca. 1150 v. chr.).* Vol. 23, 3 vols, Aegyptiaca Helvetica. Basel: Schwabe.

Douglass, M. and Isherwood, B. 1979. *The World of Goods.* New York: Routledge.

Drews, R. 1995. *The End of the Bronze Age: Changes in Warfare and the Catastrophe of ca. 1200.* Princeton: Princeton University Press.

Eaton-Krauss, M., Wagdy, A. E.-G. M., Chmeis, Z. and Lakomy, K. C. 2016. *"Der Löwe auf dem Schlachtfeld": das Grab KV 36 und die Bestattung des Maiherperi im Tal der Könige.* Wiesbaden: Reichert.

Editor. 2019. This is what American weddings look like today. *Brides* [online]: www.brides.com/gallery/american-wedding-study [accessed September 21, 2019].

Elias, J. P. and Lupton, C. 2019. Regional identification of Late Period coffins from Northern Upper Egypt. In Strudwick, H. and Dawson, J. (eds.) *Ancient Egyptian Coffins: Past – Present – Future.* Oxford: Oxbow Books, 175–184.

Emanuel, J. P. 2017. *Black Ships and Sea Raiders: The Late Bronze and Early Iron Age Context of Odysseus' Second Cretan Lie.* Lanham, MD: Lexington Books.

Eyre, C. J. 1979. *A 'Strike' Text from the Theban Necropolis. Glimpses of Ancient Egypt: Studies in Honour of H. W. Fairman.* Warminster, UK: Aris & Phillips.

Frandsen, P. J. 1990. Editing reality: the Turin Strike Papyrus. In Israelit-Groll, S. (ed.) *Studies in Egyptology Presented to Miriam Lichtheim.* Jerusalem: Magnes Press, Hebrew University, 166–99.

Gell, A. 1998. *Art and Agency: An Anthropological Theory.* Oxford: Clarendon Press.

Geßler-Löhr, B. 1981. *Ägyptische Kunst im Liebieghaus.* Frankfurt am Main: Museum alter Plastik.

Goedicke, H. and Wente, E. F. 1962. *Ostraka Michaelides*, Wiesbaden: Harrassowitz.

Grajetzki, W. 2003. *Burial Customs in Ancient Egypt: Life in Death for Rich and Poor.* London: Duckworth.

Grajetzki, W. 2007. Box coffins in the late Middle Kingdom and Second Intermediate Period. *Egitto e Vicino Oriente*, 30, 41–54.

Grajetzki, W. 2010. Class and society: position and possessions. In Wendrich, W. (ed.) *Egyptian Archaeology.* Chichester, UK: Wiley-Blackwell, 180–99.

Gutgesell, M. 1982. Die Struktur der pharaonischen Wirtshaft – eine Erwiderung. *Gottinger Miszellen*, 56, 95–109.

Gutgesell, M. 1989. *Arbeiter und Pharaonen: Wirtschafts und Sozialgeschichte im Alten Ägypten.* Hildesheim: Gerstenberg.

Haring, B. J. J. 2006. *The Tomb of Sennedjem (TT1) in Deir el-Medina: Palaeography.* Cairo: Institut français d'archéologie orientale.

Hawary, A. E. 2018. Epistemological things! Mystical things! Towards an ancient Egyptian ontology. In Moreno García, J. C., Quirke, S., Miniaci, G.

et al. (eds.) *The Arts of Making in Ancient Egypt: Voices, Images, and Objects of Material Producers 2000–1550 BC*. Leiden: Sidestone, 67–80.

Hayes, W. C. 1959. *The Scepter of Egypt: A Background for the Study of the Egyptian Antiquities in the Metropolitan Museum of Art II. The Hyksos Period and the New Kingdom (1675–1080 BC)*. Cambridge, MA: Harvard University Press for the Metropolitan Museum of Art.

Hodder, I. 2012. *Entangled: An Archaeology of the Relationships Between Humans and Things*. Malden, MA: Wiley-Blackwell.

Iacono, F. 2019. *The Archaeology of Late Bronze Age Interaction and Mobility at the Gates of Europe: People, Things and Networks Around the Southern Adriatic Sea*. London: Bloomsbury Academic.

Janssen, J. J. 1975. *Commodity Prices from the Ramesside Period*. Leiden: Brill.

Janssen, J. J. 1988. On prices and wages in Ancient Egypt. *Altorientalische Forschungen*, 15, 10–23.

Janssen, J. J. 1992. The year of the strikes. *Bulletin de la Société d'Égyptologie Genève*, 16, 41–9.

Janssen, J. J. 1997. *Village Varia: Ten Studies on the History and Administration of Deir el-Medina*. Leiden: Nederlands Instituut voor het Nabije Oosten.

Jørgensen, M. 2001. *Catalogue Egypt III. Coffins, Mummy Adornments and Mummies From the Third Intermediate, Late, Ptolemaic and the Roman Periods (1080 BC–AD 400)*. Copenhagen: Ny Carlsberg Glyptotek.

Jurman, C. 2018. To show and to designate: attitudes towards representing craftsmanship and material culture in Middle Kingdom elite tombs. In Moreno García, J. C., Quirke, S., Miniaci, G. and Stauder, A. (eds.) *The Arts of Making in Ancient Egypt: Voices, Images, and Objects of Material Producers 2000–1550 BC*. Leiden: Sidestone, 101–116.

Kanawanti, N. 2005. Decoration of burial chambers, sarcophagi and coffins in the Old Kingdom. In Bedier, S., Daoud, K. and Abd el-Fattah, S. (eds.) *Studies in Honor of Ali Radwan*. Cairo: Conseil Suprême des Antiquités.

Keller, A. C. 1984. How many draughtsmen named Amenhotep? A study of some Deir el-Medina painters. *Journal of the American Research Center in Egypt*, 21, 119–29.

Keller, A. C. 1991. Royal painters: Deir el-Medina in Dynasty XIX. In Bleiberg, E. and Freed, R. (eds.) *Fragments of a Shattered Visage: Proceedings of the International Symposium of Ramesses the Great*. Memphis: Memphis State University, 50–86.

Keller, C. A. 2001. A family affair: the decoration of Theban Tomb 359. In Davies, W. V. (ed.) *Colour and Painting in Ancient Egypt*. London: British Museum Press, 73–93.

Keller, C. A. 2003. Un artiste égyptien à l'œuvre: le dessinateur en chef Amenhotep. In Andreu, G. (ed.) *Deir el-Médineh et la Vallée des Rois: la vie en Egypte au temps des pharaons du Nouvel Empire. Actes du colloque organisé par le Musée du Louvre, les 3 et 4 mai 2002*. Paris: Khéops; Musée du Louvre, 83–114.

Kemp, B. 1991. *Ancient Egypt: Anatomy of a Civilization*, London: Routledge.

Knapp, A. B. and Manning, S. W. 2016. Crisis in context: the end of the Late Bronze Age in the Eastern Mediterranean. *American Journal of Archaeology*, 120, 99–149.

Kramer-Hajos, M. 2016. *Mycenaean Greece and the Aegean World: Palace and Province in the Late Bronze Age*. Cambridge: Cambridge University Press.

Lakomy, K. C. 2016. *Der Löwe auf dem Schlachtfeld: Das Grab KV 36 und die Bestattung des Maiherperi im Tal der Könige*. Wiesbaden: Reichert.

Latour, B. and Porter, C. 1993. *We Have Never Been Modern*. Cambridge, MA: Harvard University Press.

Latour, B. and Woolgar, S. 1986. *Laboratory Life: The Construction of Scientific Facts*. Princeton: Princeton University Press.

LeCain, T. J. 2017. *The Matter of History*. Cambridge: Cambridge University Press.

Lichtheim, M. 1975. *Ancient Egyptian Literature. Vol. I: The Old and Middle Kingdoms*. Los Angeles: University of California Press.

Lüscher, B. 1998. *Untersuchungen zu Totenbuch Spruch 151*. Wiesbaden: Harrassowitz.

Malafouris, L. 2013. *How Things Shape the Mind: A Theory of Material Engagement*. Cambridge, MA: The MIT Press.

Manassa, C. and Darnell, J. C. 2004. *The Enigmatic Netherworld Books of the Solar-Osirian Unity: Cryptographic Compositions in the Tombs of Tutankhamun, Ramesses VI and Ramesses IX*. Göttingen: Academic Press; Vandenhoeck & Ruprecht.

Mandeville, R. 2014. *Wage Accounting in Deir el-Medina*. Wallasey, UK: Abercromby Press.

McDowell, A. G. 1999. *Village Life in Ancient Egypt: Laundry Lists and Love Songs*. Oxford: Oxford University Press.

Meskell, L. 1999. Archaeologies of life and death. *American Journal of Archaeology*, 103, 181–99.

Miniaci, G., Moreno García, J. C., Quirke, S. and Stauder, A. (eds.) 2018. *The Arts of Making in Ancient Egypt: Voices, Images, and Objects of Material Producers 2000–1550 BC*. Leiden: Sidestone.

Müller, M. 2004. Der Turiner Streikpapyrus (pTurin 1880). In Wilhelm, G. and Janowski, B. (eds.) *Texte zum Rechts- und Wirtschaftsleben*. Gütersloh: Gütersloher Verlagshaus, 165–84.

Murray, S. 2017. *The Collapse of the Mycenaean Economy: Imports, Trade, and Institutions, 1300–700 BCE*. New York: Cambridge University Press.

Myśliwiec, K. 2014. The dead in the marshes: reed coffins revisited. In Jucha, M. A., Dębowska-Ludwin, J. and Kołodziejczyk, P. (eds.) *Aegyptus Est Imago Caeli: Studies Presented to Krzysztof M. Ciałowicz on His 60th Birthday*. Krakow: Institute of Archaeology, Jagiellonian University in Krakow; Archaeologica Foundation, 105–13.

Niwiński, A. 1987. Sarcophagi, stelae and funerary papyri of the Third Intermediate Period and the Late Period. In Donadoni-Roveri, A.-M. (ed.) *Egyptian Civilization: Religious Beliefs*. Milan: Electa Spa; Istituto Bancario San Paolo, 212–25.

Niwiński, A. 1987–1988. The Solar-Osirian Unity as principle of the Theology of the "State of Amen" in Thebes in the 21st Dynasty. *Jaarbericht van het Voorziatisch-Egyptisch Genootschap Ex Oriente Lux*, 30, 89–107.

Niwiński, A. 1988. *Twenty-First Dynasty Coffins from Thebes: Chronological and Typological Studies*. Mainz am Rhein: Phillip von Zabern.

Niwiński, A. 1996. Coffins from the tomb of Iurudef – a reconsideration. The problem of some crude coffins from the Memphite area and Middle Egypt. *Bibliotheca Orientalis*, 53, 324–63.

Olsen, B. 2010. *In Defense of Things: Archaeology and the Ontology of Objects*. Lanham, MD: AltaMira Press.

Onderka, P. and Toivari-Viitala, J. 2014. Eastern Cemetery reconsidered. In Onderka, P. (ed.) *The Deir el-Medina and Jaroslav Černý Collections*. Prague: National Museum.

Ostrand, K. 2013. Revisiting TT8: intact private tomb of Kha & Merit at Deir el Medina. *KMT*, 24, 18–38.

Park, A. 2019. Here's how much the average wedding in 2018 cost – and who paid, *Brides* [online]: www.brides.com/story/american-wedding-study-how-much-average-wedding-2018-cost [accessed September 21, 2019].

Parkinson, R. B. 2010. Egypt: a life before the afterlife. The *Guardian*, November 5, 2010.

Peet, T. E. 1930. *The Great Tomb-Robberies of the Twentieth Egyptian Dynasty, Being a Critical Study with Translations and Commentaries of the Papyri in Which They are Recorded*. Oxford: Clarendon Press.

Peterková Hlouchová, M. 2017. New finds from Greco-Roman Period decorated wooden coffins from Abusir South. In Dębowska-Ludwin, J., Rosińska-Balik, K., Walsh, C. and Chyla, J. M. (eds.) *Current Research in Egyptology 2016: Proceedings of the Seventh Annual Symposium; Jagiellonian University, Krakow, Poland, 4–7 May 2016*. Oxford: Oxbow Books, 136–49.

Pfoh, E. 2016. *Syria-Palestine in the Late Bronze Age: An Anthropology of Politics and Power*. Abingdon, UK: Routledge.

Quirke, S. 2013. *Going Out in Daylight – prt m hrw: The Ancient Egyptian Book of the Dead; Translation, Sources, Meaning*. London: Golden House Publications.

Raven, M. J. 1991. *The Tomb of Iurudef: A Memphite Official in the Reign of Ramesses II*. London: Egypt Exploration Society.

Raven, M. J. 2017. Third Intermediate Period burials in Saqqara. In Guichard, H. and Amenta, A. (eds.) *Proceedings First Vatican Coffin Conference 19–22 June 2013*. Vatican City: Edizioni Musei Vaticani, 419–24.

Raven, M. J., Aston, D. A., Taylor, J. H. et al. 1998. The date of the secondary burials in the Tomb of Iurudef at Saqqara. *Oudheidkundige Mededelingen uit het Rijksmuseum van Oudheden*, 78, 7–30.

Reid, D. M. 2002. *Whose Pharaohs? Archaeology, Museums, and Egyptian National Identity from Napoleon to World War I*. Los Angeles: University of California Press.

Rigault, P. and Thomas, C. 2018. The Egyptian craftsman and the modern researcher: the benefits of archeometrical analyses. In Moreno García, J. C., Quirke, S., Miniaci, G. and Stauder, A. (eds.) *The Arts of Making in Ancient Egypt: Voices, Images, and Objects of Material Producers 2000–1550 BC*. Leiden: Sidestone, 211–23.

Romer, J. 1988. Who made the private tombs of Thebes? In Lorton, B. B. A. D. (ed.) *Essays in Egyptology in Honor of Hans Goedicke*. San Antonio, TX: Van Sicklen, pp. 211–32.

Rondano, V. 2020. The economy of human resilience: exploring economic growth during political instability in Ancient Egypt. PhD thesis: University of California Los Angeles.

Sanjaume, S. I. 2006. La Tomba de Sennedjem a Deir-el-Medina TT1. PhD thesis: University of Barcelona.

Scalf, F. (ed.). 2017. *Book of the Dead: Becoming God in Ancient Egypt*, Vol. 39, Oriental Institute Museum Publications. Chicago: The Oriental Institute of the University of Chicago.

Schiaparelli, E. 1927. *La tomba intatta dell'architetto Cha. Relazione sui lavori della missione archeologica italiana in Egitto (anni 1903–1920)*. Turin: Giovanni Chiantore.

Serres, M. 1995. *Genesis*. Ann Arbor: University of Michigan Press.

Smith, M. L. 2019. *Cities: The First 6,000 Years*. New York: Viking.

Smith, S. T. 1992. Intact tombs of the Seventeenth and Eighteenth Dynasties from Thebes and the New Kingdom burial system. *Mitteilungen des*

Deutschen Archäologischen Instituts, Abteilung Kairo (DAIK) (Mainz/Cairo/ Berlin/Wiesbaden), 48, 193–231.

Smith, S. T. and Buzon, M. R. 2014a. Colonial entanglements: "Egyptianization" in Egypt's Nubian empire and the Nubian Dynasty. In Anderson, J. R. and Welsby, D. A. (eds.) *The Fourth Cataract and Beyond: Proceedings of the 12th International Conference for Nubian Studies*. Leuven: Peeters, 431–42.

Smith, S. T. and Buzon, M. R. 2014b. Identity, commemoration, and remembrance in colonial encounters: burials at Tombos during the Egyptian New Kingdom Nubian Empire and its aftermath. In Porter, B. W. and Boutin, A. T. (eds.) *Remembering the Dead in the Ancient Near East: Recent Contributions from Bioarchaeology and Mortuary Archaeology*. Boulder: University Press of Colorado, 185–215.

Spalinger, A. J. 2005. *War in Ancient Egypt: The New Kingdom*. Oxford: Blackwell.

Steiner, F. 1999. On the process of civilization. In Fardon, A. J. A. R. (ed.) *Orientpolitik, Value, and Civilization: Franz Baermann Steiner, Selected Writings II*. Oxford: Berghahn.

Strutner, S. 2015. America has more self-storage facilities than McDonald's, because apparently we're all hoarders. *Huffington Post* [online]: www.huffpost .com/entry/self-storage-mcdonalds_n_7107822 [accessed September 14, 2019].

Takahashi, K., Nishisaka, A., Abe, Y. et al. 2013. アメンヘテプ3世王墓壁画 に使用された顔料の化学分析 [Chemical analysis of the pigments used in the wall paintings of the royal tomb of Amenophis III]. *The Journal of Egyptian Studies*, 19, 58–96.

Taylor, J. H. 1985. The development of Theban coffins during the Third Intermediate Period: a typological study. Unpublished dissertation, Birmingham University.

Taylor, J. H. 1989. *Egyptian Coffins, Shire Egyptology 11*. Princes Risborough, UK: Shire Publications.

Taylor, J. H. 1999. The burial assemblage of Henutmehyt: inventory. In Davies, W. V. (ed.) *Studies in Egyptian Antiquities: A Tribute to T. G. H. James*. London: British Museum, 59–72.

Taylor, J. H. 2001. *Death and the Afterlife in Ancient Egypt*. London: British Museum Press.

Taylor, J. H. (ed.) 2010. *Journey Through the Afterlife: Ancient Egyptian Book of the Dead*. London and Cambridge, MA: British Museum Press; Harvard University Press.

Valbelle, D. 1985. *Les ouvriers de la tombe: Deir el-Médineh à l'époque ramesside, Bibliothèque d'étude 96*. Cairo: Institut français d'archéologie orientale.

Van Walsem, R. 1997. *The Coffin of Djedmonthuiufankh in the National Museum of Antiquities at Leiden*. Leiden: Nederlands Instituut voor het Nabije Oosten.

Van Walsem, R. 2000. Deir el Medina as the place of origin of the Coffin of Anet in the Vatican (Inv.: XIII.2.1, XIII.2.2). In Demarée, R. J. and Egberts, A. (eds.) *Deir el Medina in the Third Millennium AD*. Leiden: Nederlands Instituut voor het Nabije Oosten, 337–49.

Vassilika, E. (ed.) 2010. *The Tomb of Kha the Architect*. Turin and Florence: Fondazione Museo delle Antichità; Scala.

Velde, H. T. 1971. Some remarks on the structure of Egyptian divine triads. *Journal of Egyptian Archaeology*, 57, 80–6.

Wenger, E. 1998. *Communities of Practice: Learning, Meaning, and Identity*. Cambridge: Cambridge University Press.

Wengrow, D. 2006. *The Archaeology of Early Egypt: Social Transformations in North-East Africa, 10,000 to 2650 BC*. Cambridge: Cambridge University Press.

Willems, H. 1988. *Chests of Life: A Study of the Typology and Conceptual Development of Middle Kingdom Standard Class Coffins*. Leiden: Ex Oriente Lux.

Yasur-Landau, A. 2010. *The Philistines and Aegean Migration at the End of the Late Bronze Age*. New York: Cambridge University Press.

Zivie, A.-P. 2003. *Un détour par Saqqara: Deir el Médineh et la nécropole memphite. Deir el Médineh et la Vallée des Rois: La vie en Égypte au temps des pharaons du Nouvel Empire. Actes du colloque organisé par le musée du Louvre les 3 et 4 mai 2002*. Paris: Khéops; Musée du Louvre.

Cambridge Elements ☰

Ancient Egypt in Context

Gianluca Miniaci
University of Pisa

Gianluca Miniaci is Associate Professor in Egyptology at the University of Pisa, Honorary Researcher at the Institute of Archaeology, UCL – London, and Chercheur associé at the École Pratique des Hautes Études, Paris. He is currently co-director of the archaeological mission at Zawyet Sultan (Menya, Egypt). His main research interest focuses on the social history and the dynamics of material culture in the Middle Bronze Age Egypt and its interconnections between the Levant, Aegean, and Nubia.

Juan Carlos Moreno García
CNRS, Paris

Juan Carlos Moreno García (PhD in Egyptology, 1995) is a CNRS senior researcher at the University of Paris IV-Sorbonne, as well as lecturer on social and economic history of ancient Egypt at the École des Hautes Études en Sciences Sociales (EHESS) in Paris. He has published extensively on the administration, socio-economic history, and landscape organization of ancient Egypt, usually in a comparative perspective with other civilizations of the ancient world, and has organized several conferences on these topics.

Anna Stevens
University of Cambridge and Monash University

Anna Stevens is a research archaeologist with a particular interest in how material culture and urban space can shed light on the lives of the non-elite in ancient Egypt. She is Senior Research Associate at the McDonald Institute for Archaeological Research and Assistant Director of the Amarna Project (both University of Cambridge).

About the Series

The aim of this Elements series is to offer authoritative but accessible overviews of foundational and emerging topics in the study of ancient Egypt, along with comparative analyses, translated into a language comprehensible to non-specialists. Its authors will take a step back and connect ancient Egypt to the world around, bringing ancient Egypt to the attention of the broader humanities community and leading Egyptology in new directions.

Cambridge Elements ≡

Ancient Egypt in Context

Elements in the Series

Printed in the United States
by Baker & Taylor Publisher Services

Printed in the United States
by Baker & Taylor Publisher Services